Paradigms
of a
Broken Mind

Paradigms of a Broken Mind

Alexandria Linnae

For those who inspire me,
hearts that can't sleep
and minds that dream deep.

Introduction

This collection spans twenty years of my life. For the longest time, these words lived within scraps of paper, tucked away in shoe boxes, or buried in the notes on my phone. I never considered putting them all into a book until recently, but once the idea took hold, I couldn't let it go. I wanted to bring these words together into something tangible—something I could hold in my hands and say, *This is me. I made this.*

But this book is more than just a collection of poetry. It is a release—a way to finally let go of the pain that once held me captive, keeping me bound to suffering. After all these years, I have processed the hurt and confusion, and now I am ready to move forward. Some of these words no longer reflect how I feel, while others still resonate deeply.

Writing has always been my rawest form of expression—unfiltered, unprocessed, created in the heat of the moment. Often, I wouldn't even understand how I felt until I saw the words staring back at me from the page. This process has been both my refuge and my revelation, allowing me to make sense of emotions I didn't always have the words for.

At its core, this book is for me—a symbolic closing of one chapter and an opening to whatever comes next. But it is also for you, the reader, and for anyone who finds comfort or inspiration in these words—or even just a moment of reflection. I have poured myself into these pages, and I ask that you approach them with gentleness, knowing they hold pieces of a person who was searching, questioning, and feeling deeply.

This book is a journey through five chapters, each exploring a distinct theme: depression, abstract thoughts, the world and society, love and heartbreak, and sex.
Many of the pieces within this collection hold layered meanings, with some revealing entirely different interpretations depending on how they are read. Even the contents page holds meaning beyond what it seems—perhaps you'll notice!

I hope this book reminds you to pause, to breathe, and to observe the world around you. I hope it encourages you to think more, question more, feel more, and never lose sight of what truly matters.

Thank you for reading.

Contents

Sinking Under

Leeches

It's like a part of me's addicted to the pain,
like a leech is stuck to my brain,
and with every thought that I think
it gets stronger, while I'm getting weak.

They say to keep my head up and be strong,
that it's a moment, it won't last too long.
But they've been wrong,
it's always been here.
This moment has been my lifetime.
It's not getting better, I say.

I want to be picked apart
like a flower in the hands of a curious child.
P l u c k by p l u c k by p l u c k.
I want every crevasse to be opened,
every breath recorded,
I want to know *why* I'm designed this way.

Why I can't be happy
even when I lie to myself
and say that I am?
Why was I made this way?

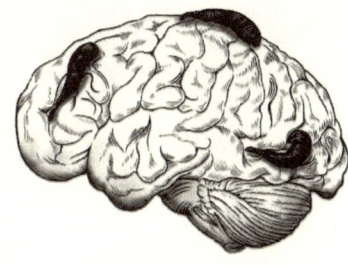

3

To Be an Artist

I'm happy to be an artist.
Happy to bear the pain.
Happy to share my deepest wounds.
Happy to be called insane.

I'm happy to live unfiltered,
tethered to tides and rain.
Happy to be unsettled.
Happy to spill my vein.

I couldn't imagine not being an artist,
to share and teach and love,
to create different realities
than the ones we're shown hereof.

I'd happily expose myself, and turn it into art
if it meant that someone else out there
could feel it in their heart,
and know they're not alone,
that I can feel it too.

Everything that I create in time,
It's always been for you.

2 A.M.

Two a.m.
Too deep,
Too void…
To fill.

Misery

Is that what it takes to write?
Then, I'd better be miserable for the rest of my life.
Better find pain at the end of a knife,
better not ever become a wife.
Misery—
Such a miserable word.
Without it, some great things would've never occurred.
It's sad that it's so hard to write when I'm happy,
'cause who the hell wants to always sound sappy
just to express themselves?

Deals From Underneath

I feel my body eating itself
little by little each day.
The rumbling in my stomach
reminds me I've yet to eat today.
But somehow, I don't feel hungry,
the emptiness keeps me full.
Just as the silence is louder than any sound—
I wish you'd talk to me.

My body is turning inside out,
I'm living in my truth,
living in this aging youth,
alone inside this booth.

A booth inside the walls of hell
I never thought I'd see again.
They ask me what my order is
and force-feed me all my sin.

Again, again, again,
I am living on repeat.
I should have never bargained
with the devil underneath.

One Line

A druggie with a brain, just trying to maintain,
nose full of cocaine, cause the soul's in pain.

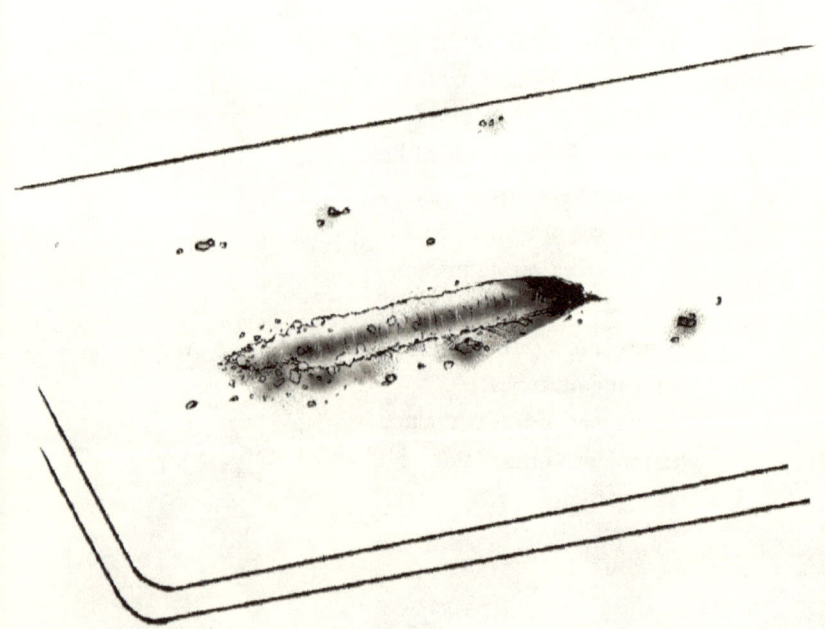

No Way Home

Cruising, looking for trouble.
Things are just too simple,
someone popped my bubble.
I'm living a dream,
I'm living in circles,
feel like a sim,
wandering in circles.
Cruising around
'cause I lose my temper.
Can't tell you what happened,
I'm losing my tender.
Losing my sweet.
There's blood on my back
and glass in my feet,
tears in my eyes
I've neglected to meet.
It's all just a game,
deceit, deceit.

Loner

Alone is where I am.
Finally, somewhere I know.
I've been gone for way too long,
putting faith in I don't know.

Alone is where I'm happy,
where I'm comfortable and free.
Alone is somewhere I can think,
somewhere I can feel me.

Alone is always peaceful,
even when it's sad.
Alone is where I long to be,
the safe space I've always had.

Alone is how I grow,
where I practice what I know.
Alone is all I need right now,
I hope you understand.

Truth

When I go to the bathroom to put my face on,
it isn't makeup I'm referring to.

It's the face of acceptance I've so easily mastered
so that I may smile at you today,
knowing that last night I cried in the bathroom
with all the lights off,
wondering what it'd be like to end my life.

You accept my smile,
but would never accept my truth.

Scenes From My Head

Remnants of white powder linger on the coffee table,
Traces of her lipstick kiss the empty glass,
Lighters sprawled across the floor, the air humming
with smoky breath,
All this just to keep a smile, or to make the time pass.

Crying for a Century

Can anybody hear me?
Can anybody hear my cries?
I've been crying for a century,
it's hard to wipe my eyes.

Can anybody see me?
Do you see behind my eyes
that I'm screaming, and I'm bleeding
from the depths of my insides?

I don't want to be a burden,
so I smile, and I dance.
I sing though no one's listening,
it's my shot at a chance.

I just want to feel alive,
tired of this hidden mess.
I thought I'd found the answers
to pull me out of this distress.

But I guess I lost my balance.
Somehow, the rug was pulled from under me.
And now I'm aching on the floor
saying, "Pretty please, surrender me"

To death—
To anywhere but here.
The walls are closing in on me,

I'm suffocating in fear
of all my failures,
my undermined attempts
at doing what I love
to keep my head high, up above
all this underlying pain
I thought that I'd forgotten.
Now it's catching up to me,
I feel so damn rotten
and misused,
mentally abused.
I've been holding up for years and years
but now I'm getting weak.

My beams are rotten
from the waves of my despair.
The way I'm feeling now
seems like I'm beyond repair—
and who's to care?

I'm alone inside this world.

Every helping hand has hit me too.
It's no wonder that I bite.
I am a person,
not a pretty wind-up doll.
You say that you're here to catch me
while hoping secretly I fall.
So now I've fallen,
and I'm stuck, I can't get up.

The sheets placed on my bed
pull me in, man, what the fuck—
Just let me go!

I don't want to be a victim,
another body left to burn.
I'm looking in the mirror,
wondering, "Will it be my turn?"

My Safe Haven

I am repeatedly shown love
in a world that's felt so dark.
So dark that when I do feel love
I question if it's real.
I get surprised when people care,
elated when people share,
parts of themselves I know to be true.

My whole life, people have wanted
something from me.
So much so, I've grown weary.

I've been gawked at, lusted over, used, and lied to.
I've been given countless kisses
by men who've turned and thrown me down,
pushed me and abused me,
grabbed my neck and ripped my gown.

I've been followed home and stalked,
even from a different state.
Dressed in silk and compliments
that served merely as the bait—
to someone's true intention.
And with so much attention,
I never know what's real.
Seems like every smile has its own hidden deal.

So, you question why I run,

why I isolate myself,
why I deal with everything alone—
adding weight to the shelf,
piling in my mind,
it's okay, I'm fine.
But really, I'd just rather be alone.

Sad

Are you sad?
Like, I am sad?
Does it leak from your soul?
Pouring from within,
Leaves the depths of you hollow.

The Taste of Forgetting

Poison, filtering through my veins,
I say that I'm alright, yet I drink like I'm in pain.
One tequila, two tequila, three tequila, four…
I say that I can't feel 'em, so I drink and drink some more,
until it finally hits me, and I wind up on the floor,
or in somebody's bed, with a hand around my head.

I'm walking in my mind, but I keep falling down,
'cause there's holes in my memory,
like there's tears in my gown.
And I never play the victim 'cause I know who I AM.
And I take responsibility, unlike every other man.

But just because I'm strong enough to deal
doesn't mean that I should,
carry all the weight
that no one else ever could.
ME TOO.
But I've never said the words,

I've always taken the blame.
I let them get away,
just so they could play,
find another prey,
it's not okay—

Waking up with no memory,
hearing the words of last night

but not recognizing the melody,
of your own tune.

And yet you danced the night away,
twirling and twirling, hoping that you'd spin away.
It's all just fun.
At least it was until it ended.
Why did you drink so much
just to end up apprehended
in the arms of a stranger?
It's yourself you reprehend.

But you keep drinking—
To forget, or to remember?
Either way, it's been wrong, and to this,
I surrender.

What it Takes to Feel

For the ones that never had a part of me,
I'm sorry.
I used you all like cattle just to fill my empty hole.
Not knowing my destruction
was in vitro,
soon to be birthed through me,
leaves a leak in my soul.

I've tried to hide my sorrows
under bottles and bodies whole.
Thinking I could change my composition
from being weak to being cold.

But I was never weak,
in fact, I was stronger then,
'cause I loved with all my heart
and still had soul, the perfect zen.

Now I'm too "strong" to be affected
when I share with you my sin,
but when longing becomes lonely
I'm reminded I can't win.

Digging holes for my affection
to lie underneath the surface,
I fall slowly into memories of
what it's like to have a purpose.

It's so easy not to feel,
but what I stray from, always eats at me.
I'm a fruit constantly peeled,
left to rot in my own hands.
I cry.
It's all my fault again.
I've been doing this too long,
why can't I bring it to an end?
It's pain now or later, but later takes longer to heal.
At least for now, I'll know what it's like to feel real.

Metamorphosis

I was always the girl who loved too deep,
who never, ever went to sleep.
The girl who'd sit and watch the stars,
lying on top of dusty cars.

I was always the one to take the blame,
yet leave nothing attached to my name.
The one who'd fake her every smile,
walk to you, despite the miles.

I was always the girl who hid.
I could do without attention.
All eyes fixated on me,
my body tight with hypertension.

I was always the girl to question
even my own reflection.
The actions of my peers
seemed to have no direction.

I was always the one to cry
alone beneath my sheets,
wishing I could go away,
get lost and feel complete.

I was that girl, though no one knew,
cause no one ever saw me.
I was a girl covered in blue

wishing you'd hear my plea.

But no one ever did.
They accepted my veneer.
And when I begged to die,
my voice, no one could hear.

I remember though—it's clear.

This girl within my memory.
I remember her as me.

I wish that you could see
how it took that pain to be me—
to become this very essence.

I picked up all the pieces,
carried her on my back
until she had the strength
to build up an attack.

I REMEMBER DYING—
then flooding back with life.
Accepting all the pain.
Accepting all the strife.

I remember feeling new,
unsure of what to do.
With all this newfound happiness,
I wondered if it was true.

Could this still be me—
the same untethered girl
who finally found a way
to make it in this world?

I remember smiling,
and finally feeling good—
even about the way I looked.
I'm so misunderstood.

I began to trot
on this journey of self-love,
and finally understand
what it means to be above—

Not above anyone, but above everything
that weighed so heavily on top of me.

Above my defeat,
above the gum on your feet,
and above the false guarantee
that there was ever something
wrong with me.

I smile now without hiding my face.
There are no longer memories I wish to erase.
I live now and feel so complete.
And wonder how I could have ever been beat.

Some look at me now
and would never have known
I once was a girl who felt so alone.

We all perceive each other differently,
in ways we'll never fully understand.
But never assume and never brand
another based on how they look.

Like judging a book,
bound to be mistook,

Reach for the tether,
and undo the hook.

Phases of the Moon

You say that it takes strength to feel,
    but somehow, I feel that's untrue.
    For history has passed, and all great leaders
    seem to attest to the rule—

That feelings hinder the mind,
    cloud it all up, and waste time.
    Feelings make me feel weak.
    I can't even move from my sheets.

How can you say this is strength?
    I stand at the end of my length.
    Waiting to jump, it feels calm,
    the warmth shriveled up in my palm.

I hate that I feel so incapable,
    like something chewed holes in my brain.
    The thoughts in my mind untranslatable,
    you can't even see I'm in pain.

To feel simply feels like a curse,
    in a world that is taught to coerce.
    Give up your pride, sell your soul;
    we'll fill you with lies till you're whole.

I'm stuck between waning and aiming,
    lost between waxing and axing
    my own golden head on a platter,
    Is that what this dim world is asking?

'Cause I can't wake up from this cycle.
    I've tried over and over again.
    The wall's closing in on my skull.
    It repeats: the defeat of my zen.

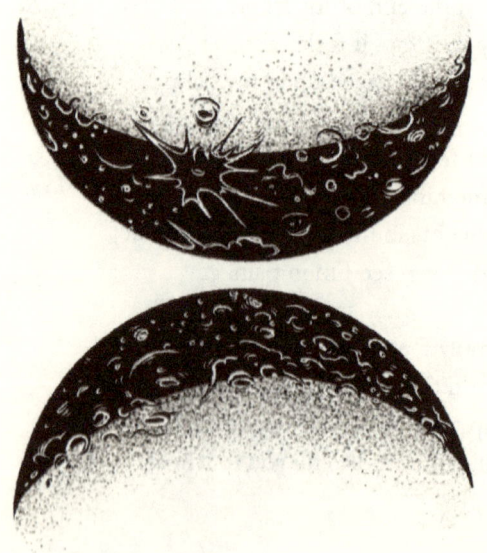

A Diamond or a Fly

I feel like a waste of potential,
a waste of beauty and intelligence.
I feel like a waste of a person
who was never supposed to be.
So many lives to have lived before me
so that I could take this space.
So many events to have happened,
for me to exist in this time and place.

Yet, I still cannot find a reason
to be happy I'm alive.
Still can't understand
why someone as gifted as me
won't thrive.
No matter how hard I try,
every day I want to die.
And I wonder why it is I was created.
Against all odds I beat to be here,
why me?

Sometimes, I feel like a diamond,
buried deep in the ground,
unable to dig myself up and out.
Finding ways to push
with every movement of the earth,
until I can feel the surface.
Or until someone can see a glimmer in the dust
and set me free.

Other times, I feel
like a fly on the wall,
absorbing it all
but utterly useless to most of the world.
Sometimes, I know I'm great,
then question if that's my ego
comforting me for being average.
Telling me lies so that I feel special
enough to keep on.

Why do I long to be different and unique?
Or is it that's just how I feel, because I am—
Different.
Unique.
Lonely.
Misunderstood.

Or is it just my brain
struggling to maintain
some sort of balance?
I don't enjoy being sad.
But I've never felt a day without the rain.

Perfection

I think I'm struggling with these ideas of perfection—
reaching towards an unattainable goal.
And even though I know there's nothing
on the other side,
I keep pushing, reaching, thinking
once I get there,
I'll be whole.
I've lived my life with no room for mistakes,
then wonder why I'm still stuck
in this small space.
The more I grow, the more I realize
I...can't...breathe—
Within these walls that leave no room
for me to be at peace.

I feel like growing; I feel I'm growing now.
No longer able to be held
inside perfection.
No longer willing to be locked
inside this spotless glass.
No longer letting you examine me
to see if I will pass.
I ate perfection.
So much, it backed me up.
Now I'm so full of it, I can't enjoy the taste
of anything *perfect* anymore.

Floating

I feel as if I'm floating,
just waiting on a wave to carry me home.
Waiting isn't something I'm good at…
Probably why I'm always left to roam.
I used to be in charge of the sails,
every aspect of my life was planned.
But the wind always had other plans,
which is why I've decided to just let go,
softly, as the wind carries me home.

Maybe it's a reset button,
maybe it's what I need.
Maybe I traveled too far down a path not meant for me.

I'm tired of feeling lost,
broken, and in pain,
as if I don't work properly.
Tired of being chased
by people who don't have what it takes
to love me.
Tired of being misunderstood,
viewed as something that isn't me.
Tired of being me,
ready for the next life version.
Again and again, I end up here.
What is it that I'm missing?

A Life With No Vice

I've always felt a little alone and misunderstood,
but today, I feel exceptionally lonely.
The kind of loneliness that creeps up and envelopes you,
pulling you down into darkness.
The kind of loneliness where you can't even hear
the words, or feel the touch of a friend.
Loneliness that's so thick it's almost hard to breathe.
Loneliness that clouds your vision,
until alone is all you see.
I'm lonely.
And for the first time in my life, I am sitting with that.
Sitting with the discomfort,
instead of picking up the phone and reaching out
to a body
that will warm my flesh,
ease the distress.
I am choosing to be alone,
because sometimes that's what you need
instead of suffocating greed.
Being wrapped in the arms of someone
is never guaranteed
to make you feel less lonely.
More times than not, the wrong person makes you feel
even more alone.

A bone with no flesh.
A skin with no soul.

Empty bones in a ruin—

When you know that you don't love them.

For the first time in a long time
I am feeling everything,
with no vice to call my own.
For the first time in a long time
I am home—
and tending to my wounds.

Pain's Game

I used to be addicted to the pain,
watch the blood drip from in me, let it drain.

I used to think that pain was in my name,
that without it, I wouldn't be the same.

I used to tell my brain that I deserved it,
that somewhere along the years, I had earned it.

I used to treat the pain as a reward,
turn my cut-up words into a chord.

I used to say the pain would make me stronger,
and with that strength, I'd live longer.

The resilience to pain would make me fearless,
'cause if I always bounced back, what would I fear?

I ate my pain until it killed me—
And when I woke, I saw it true.
The pain had left, and there was nothing.
Not even that tearful color blue.

That pain I hated, taught me love,
and made me everything I am.
I found a way to see its beauty,
transform its power into a plan.

Time Heals Not

I have a little secret to tell,
it might not make you feel very well—
They say that it gets better,
that all is healed with time,
but after so many harrowing years,
I think that's a lie.

I've held on all this time,
with hope it might be true,
that if I just kept pushing,
I'd see something more than blue.

Every year is different,
but inside, I'm still the same—
Aching with a heart
that remembers every name.

Remembers every love,
Remembers all the pain.

And it's hard to admit
that it doesn't get better.
In fact, it might get worse.
For those who are optimistic,
I'm sorry for the curse
of reading these words.

Although, maybe you'll be fine

and get to see the other side.
Maybe I'm afflicted
with a different type of mind.

I wish I felt more,
I wish I felt less.

I wish that for a moment
I could breathe—
And know that I'm... happy
on the other side.

Dreams

End Scene

Drip…
Drip…
Bright red falls on a bed of white snow.
The beauty in death is the art of letting go

Trip

Seasons changing, colors fading,
white snow falls beneath her nose.
Kisses linger on her skin.
Petals fall from her sweet rose.

Innocent in stature, deadly with her stare.
Makes you ask the question as to what is really there.
Grabs you with a glance, traps you with her tongue.
Sets your soul into a trance, now what have you become?

Lost inside your mind? Or deep inside of hers?
Senses overlapping, taste the warmth within your palm.
Sounds are getting brighter, feel the way they smell.
Caught in a dimension, spiraling in parallel.

Bodies become lifeless, soul begins to thrive.
In this moment, everything you think becomes alive.
Energy transformed, finds its place to hide.
Pours into your body as it takes you for a ride.

Pulse begins to flicker, body starts to quiver.
Electric tickles send a rhythm shivering up your spine.
Space is closing in, time is losing shape.
Now you're lost, wondering if you'll find a quick escape.

Silence fills the air, shadows take their place.
Consciousness calls quietly
You answer, "Yes, who's there?"

Snap back to reality—

Confused with where you are,
somehow home, but feels as if you've traveled somewhere
far.
Far away from here, on a different sphere.
Caught in light as if you took a trip within a star.

Look into the mirror, tell me what you see.
You take a glance and realize you've been staring into me.

A Gift for the Moon

Are you who I think you are?
Watching from afar?
I've gazed upon your beauty,
You've outshone all of the stars.
The brightest in the sky,
Colors change with your emotions.
Dancing through the night,
Your light, an essence for our potions.
My moon, my sweet Luna,
Let me call upon your light
To lead me through the darkest times,
I need you in this fight
To master all these dreams and wishes,
Bring me to new heights.
And there with you, I'll sit and share
Our ultimate delight.

You Promised Me

Shadows on a ceiling,
visions in a cloud,
in everything I see
the answer's never heard aloud.

I could be flying on a plane
or sitting on a train,
either way, it doesn't matter,
'cause the shit's always the same.

It's hard to sort it out
when everything's tied up in knots.
Just like it's hard to shoot a vein
when everyone's filled up with clots.

But still, somehow I always manage
just to make it out alive.
Everything that's in my mind
keeps me pushing to survive.

I'm always up at night
trying to make sense of existence—
I've probably seen a thousand shooting stars
in pure consistence.
I wanted to say world,
but that's a tricky little rhyme—
I swirled, and twirled, and whirled
until my toes curled and I hurled—

Not really, but I tried.
You see, it wasn't hard,
but then again, that line of mine
won't win me an award.

But back to how I feel,
before I lose my place,
I've been rhyming since I was
a little girl without a case.

Now look where I'm at,
lost without a cause.
Looking for an easy way to
put my life on pause,
'cause I'm focused on the flaws
of everything that was,
but I'm still hoping, and I'm trying,
so just give me an applause.

Damn, that felt good.
But if only you knew,
that everything inside of me
is just trying to break through.
But you don't have a clue,
you just know my life is blue.
But there's something really wrong with me,
just like a missing screw.
And I don't know what to do,
I need a rescue.
But all this pride in me
won't let me take a hand from even you.

They say that loneliness is a virtue,
but I can't see how it's true.
But then again, maybe without it
we would lose the value.
Shit, I don't know,
I'm just waiting on a cue.
I'm just trying to go somewhere,
but I don't know where to.
And at the same time, I'm just trying to
find a way to pursue—
Everything that I believe in,
everything I want to be.
Give me something to believe in,
show me that there's more to see.
Prove there's something to put faith in,
tell me that there's more to me—
Or slowly let me down
and sink away into the sea,
end up saying sorry.

You're not the first to wear the crown
and I bet you're not the last,
but I'll just have to watch you drown
and end up part of history's past.

Voices in my head
telling me there's something different.
Saying, "You promised me you would never change."
But a lot of shit went wrong.
And the world's constantly changing.
Spinning on its axis all the while,

while I'm aging,
I'm remaining strong.
Don't tell me that I've changed,
'cause with all the shit I've been through
how can one remain unchanged?
You would think I'd be deranged,
and maybe that I am,
'cause I've been a bit estranged,
but I'm still true to who I am.

"You promised me you would never change."
And I tell you that I haven't.
But still, you're searching for some proof
that a part of me is absent.

Crazy where your mind can wander when you let it.
The people up at night are the ones who understand it.
The misfits, the loners, the complex stoners—
The ones who wash it all away until they're in their zoners.
The late-night moaners.
Now tell me, which am I?
Shit, I've been asking lots of questions
yet I still do not know why—

Why do I keep trying, to fill this empty hole
with substances and people that I know won't make me
whole?
Maybe it's because I know there's more to just this life.
Or maybe it's because I know I'll never be a wife.

But damn, who cares?

I know that it's not you,
but then again, maybe everything you said was true.
But oh well, boo hoo,
there's nothing we can do.
"You promised me you would never change."
But you promised me too.

Reconciliation

I wish that I could reconcile
my relationship with time.
For the longest I abused it,
thinking it'd always be there.
Not treating it as special,
just a frivolous affair.
When the truth is that it's precious,
I might even call it rare.
The gift of time we overlook,
just because we're unaware.

When we're young, we think forever
is a million miles away.
Not knowing that the end is racing
hastily our way.
All the time that I've spent waiting
on someone to change their ways,
or the time that I spent hoping,
instead of acting out my days.

How I wish I'd put more boundaries
around my precious time.
Not letting it be wasted
on fools with paradigms,
of what my time is worth,
and just how I should spend it.

If I could do it all again

I'd never waste a million years.
I might spend most time alone
holding on to souvenirs
of better company and atmospheres—
Where time was but a moment of appreciation
and not an eye on the clock,
counting the seconds until I can be free again.

Analyzed Lie

Trapped inside my mind.
Lost inside a dream.
Caught in a reality
that isn't what it seems.
Wandering in circles.
Greeting strangers' eyes.
Smiling, chatting, laughing,
all pointless hidden lies.
Feelings I can't feel.
Thoughts I shouldn't think.
I'm convinced there's something more,
this creation's missing link.
Or maybe it's not missing,
but somewhere in disguise.
Or maybe we're not meant to
sit and overanalyze.

Tales of a Bird

I've been meaning to sit down and do this for a while,
so long that my thoughts are now thrown in a pile.

A pen in my hand makes it all become clear.
Pen to the hand, like music to the ear.

I guess as we age, life takes its toll,
and it's hard to find time to please your soul.

But I make it my goal to never lose sight
of things that I love, the things that bring light.

I know I'm not perfect, but shit, who is?
I don't have secrets, but I do have his.

Am I wrong for the fact that I'm not always right?
Was it wrong for Eve to tell Adam, "Take a bite?"

I've been stuck in my ways,
but I'm still making moves.
I get lost in my days,
but they always improve.

My heart, it bleeds black
'cause I'm colder than night.
And I never look back
'cause I know that I might

Forget to look ahead again.
I've been there before,
but that was back then.

I feel like I'm lost, but I know that I'm not.
I was meant to just wander,
never stay in one spot.

But what about the ones who say they love me?
Will I leave them behind if they can't keep up?

I'm as free as a bird,
you can look but don't touch.
And you might hear me sing,
'cause I sing too much.

But don't get too attached
to that bird in the sky.
'Cause what's a bird gonna do?
A bird's gonna fly.

Coin Toss

So quickly, everything's changed.
Why hold on to anything,
if in the end, it's all the same?
A fleeting feeling, a darting pain,
an endless summer, filled with rain.

I thought I had the key,
held it, grasped it in my hand.
So sure that I had made it,
walking towards the promised land.

Determined, still, and faithful,
I put up a jarring fight.
Until the very end,
but it was you who blocked my sight.

Warned by the psychic,
keen as can be,
they said to watch out,
too many eyes after me.

Ojos malvados,
they watch me in my sleep,
grabbing from my plate,
so there's nothing left to eat.

Starved, bitter, angry,
like a beggar on the street.

Too proud to ask for help,
charred ashes on my feet.

Walking the gates of hell
where the fallen angels lay.
Wondering what they did,
forgot again to pray.

Smoky and dusky,
the air so thick.
It gets hard for me to breathe,
fumes are making me sick.

A burning, a hunger, so deep in my bones.
Hearts so hard, you'd think they turned to stone.

A flip of a coin,
a fork in the road.
Fate pushes on,
destiny erodes.

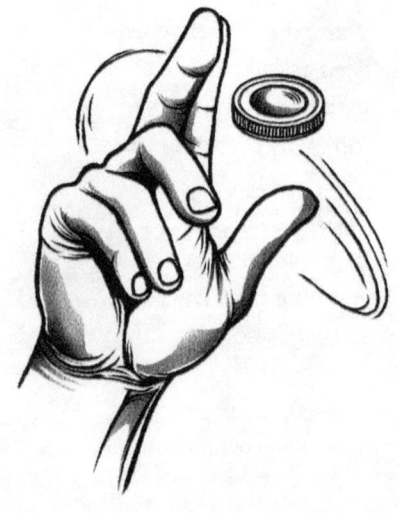

Hunting the Truth

I left the evidence right out for you.
I wanted you to know.
So you could finally catch a scent on me,
like leaving footprints in the snow.

The Crook

I've been shook by a crook!
I can tell you no lies.
I was caught on a hook,
lured by sweet lullabies.
And it pained me to look
in his dull-colored eyes.
But the something he took
was much more than a prize.
I could not overlook
our last time for goodbyes.
I've been shook by a crook!
There was no compromise.
Just an end to a book,
an untoward demise.

Distraction

Why can't I write?
I ask myself, "Why?" 'cause it's just not the same.
Old words I recite
Yet it's me who's the only one that I can blame.
Soft skin, take a bite
And assure yourself that she's not one you can tame.
Take her to a new height.
All she wants is to truthfully say that she's came.
But don't be polite,
behind closed doors, there is no shame.
She'll put up a fight,
have you question if life is truly a game.
Inside, you'll ignite.
And you'll dance right into her inviting flame.

Bed of Sin

Another day stuck in this piercing hell,
a catatonic trance.
Into the fire, I quickly fell,
and I took the devil's dance.

Lost inside a helpless world,
surrounded by remorse,
I watch the bodies as they twirl,
languishing, without a force.

Into the day, I hesitate,
to leave my webbed abyss,
'cause every day's the same old fate
I'm left to reminisce.

Gliding through the open air
I feel so out of place.
All of this I cannot bear,
just look upon my face.

The pain I swallow day by day
falls into my core.
I'm searching for another way,
an exit out the door.

You look at me and only hope,
that I would crack a smile,
but sadly, all I do is mope,

and I've become so vile.

You touch my skin and feel a chill
when once I was so warm,
but now my cold and lifeless hand
with yours can't even form.

And in the night, I stay alive
and watch the hours fade.
The sense of life I can't derive,
my heart's pressed on a blade.

I fall into an endless trap
of suffocating guilt.
Between me and my happiness is the gap
I've somehow built.
I wish I could unscrew the cap
before I slowly wilt,
but time is ticking, and I'm alone
wrapped inside my shameful quilt.

With my eyes, at you I look
and speak with calm desire.
You catch on, and bite the hook,
chasing me into the fire.

You kiss my lips, and in the bed
you slowly feel my skin.
I look at you and see the red,
the tension building from within.

I push you down, you lay your head
I feel it kicking in.
I slide on top, and in your ear breathe,
"Welcome to my bed of sin."

Double Edged

Desire me… Inspire me…
One just isn't enough.
Take time to see inside of me,
my skin's become too tough.

Don't read between the lines,
I promise there's nothing there.
Read behind the eyes,
find what's hidden, bare.

A glimpse into a fantasy
no one would know exists.
Locked without a key.
Clenched in a stone fist.

How could one ever know
how deep another feels?
An ocean hidden beneath snow,
guarding fluorescent eels.

This is the world I live in.
Constantly split in two.
Living on the borderline
of what is me and what is you.

Eagerly tipping the edge,
finger held up to a mirror,
pushing past its boundaries,

it all becomes so clear.

Dimensions frozen in time.
Time escaping space.
Takes me back into the prime,
such a familiar place.

Desire me… Inspire me…
My mind's become too tame.
Colors fading rapidly,
don't let me lose the flame.

Caught within a world like this
it's easy to lose sight.
Visions that I reminisce,
I wish I could rewrite.

Desire me… Inspire me…
Or else I'll get too bored.
Hanging on to one last pawn
before I take the board.

Desire me… Inspire me…
There's much to be explored.
Looking through your hazel eyes,
you know that you're adored.

But just desire me… Inspire me…
Don't let me end the game.
'Cause once I make that move
I won't remember your sweet name.

Desire me…Inspire me…
I slowly draw my sword,
waiting for your final move,
begging for the reward.

Fine Lines

Wine me, dine me, 69 me, intertwine your lips with mine.

Eyes combine, we recline, hips align, now touch my spine.

Misdefine, borderline, redefine, so divine.

Unleash

Lately, I've been feeling like I'm lost in a maze,
smoke in this haze, I'm caught in a daze.
Trying not to slip back into my old ways,
I'm hoping these times are just part of a phase.

But what is a phase when this world is a lie?
If but nothing else, I hope to defy
all that's become of this sick lullaby.
Your mind I'm aiming to occupy,
for the sole reason to purify.

Take your eyes off the prize and set them to the truth.
Focus on the youth.

Times aren't changing, they're just getting worse.
Just like a curse—
waiting to be untethered, waiting to be dispersed.
Preparations for the culprit who soon will immerse,
and unleash his rain unto the universe.

Like a loose cannon, I'm ready to explode!
So, they test me, and test me, hoping I'll decompose…
But I know just how to keep myself composed.
My composure's the key, I'm forever enclosed.

Take a look at my life, and it seems to be normal,
but look in between and you'll see I'm a portal.

What I hold in my mind is forever unattainable.
The key, on me, forever unexplainable.

Trapped in a body, trapped on an earth.
My soul's a monody,
just waiting to be heard.

Open your eyes, and don't be deceived.
Remember, not all is as it is perceived.

Vampire

Into the night I dwell,
my first and only home,
the darkness that has birthed me
guides me as I roam.

The scent of your sweet flesh
lingers in the air,
tickling all my senses,
resisting is a dare.

My body's urged with hunger,
I'm hunting for my prey.
A trap set just to lure you,
can't let you get away.

You tell me that you want it,
but little do you know,
the only way you'll please me
is if you're bleeding slow.

The beating of your heart
echoes through my skull,
reminding me of life
and what it's like to feel full.

To feel your warming pulse
just makes the urge intense.
One act on my impulse

and you'll be drained, without defense.

I bite you for a second,
but quickly pull away.
Your blood's left rushing towards the surface,
my thirst put on delay.

You grab my skin and then begin
to feel me from within,
I grab the blade, my conscience fades,
I press down and invade.

I feel the red, and taste it,
as it seeps from in your vein.
You squeeze me tight, and push into me,
trying to fight the pain.

My senses heighten,
life begins to flood within my brain.
You fuck me harder, as I feed,
my world's become insane.

I suck what's left, the night is ending, bodies satisfied.
The sun awakens, I say goodbye, into the day I hide.

Murderous Thoughts

I am a murderer.
I'm the worst kind.
I'll shoot you even though I know you're blind.

I am a murderer.
You'll have no choice.
My word's the only way.
You have no voice.

I am a murderer.
I'll take it slow.
I'll suck the life within until it flows…
right into me.

I'll make you feel alive, make you feel complete.
Until I rip you up and laugh at your defeat.

I'll hang you out to dry.
I'll cut you loose.
I'll squeeze until you cry,
you know it's true.

'Cause I am a murderer.
I feel no pain.
I'll feed on yours until you tell me you're *insane*.

I am a murderer.
I'll steal your soul.

You'll think you're finally whole
until I show you more.

I am a murderer.
Just STAY AWAY!
One foot into my ring and you become my prey.

On Go

Numb to life's emotions,
familiar with death's potions,
hanging on a single thread
while diving in Earth's oceans.

That's the way I seem to live,
always in such motion.

Heaven Awakes

Surrounded by billions,
yet always alone.
In this world you'll gain millions,
but might lose your soul.

With each step that we take,
we're just getting further.
Even heaven is faked,
but shhh, don't disturb her.
You might make her shake.
You don't want to stir her,
'cause then she might wake,
it'll all be a blur.
All these dreams that she'll make,
you'll never concur.
But it's hell that she'll break,
and truth will emerge.

Just look at the earth
and how the world turns.
Look at the sun
and watch how it burns.
There's more to this living
than you'll ever learn.
There's more life in giving,
and more that you'll earn.

We're floating in time,
surrounded by space.
Committing our crimes
without any face.
This life is sublime,
if we'd just embrace,
enter our prime,
and exit the race.

'Cause where are we going?
Nobody knows.
But I can show you where the rabbit hole goes—

Don't look with your eyes
'cause you'll never see.
Instead, realize
that you are the key.

Soul

It's the soul that gives purpose to the skin.

Uma Dica

Remember the softness,
the senses.
Don't forget that you are a part of everything.
Every cell. Alive. Stop to feel.

Where we get lost is in forgetting to feel.
Forgetting to breathe.
Forgetting to pay attention to each part of the world
around us. To each part of us.

I'm reminded why I dive so deep, why I'm constantly
searching and running towards something—
Towards the feeling of *feeling*.

Everything around us might be fake, might be
structured—unnaturally
But inside, we still have the choice and the power to be
free.

In your own mind.

I watched the mist from my diffuser, and everything was
calm. I saw the mist dance like a ballerina,
swaying with the breeze from the fan.

I gently laid my hand in front to feel the air, the mist.

I felt each drop of moisture in the air touch each of my individual pores. The slightest movement and the slightest breath changing the way the mist blew.
Reminding me how energies are so subtle,
so delicate.
It doesn't take much
to cause ripples—
Waves.
Energy travels fast.
And we are all connected.
Over and over and over again,
the message has always been—
That we are CONNECTED.
Always seeking CONNECTION.

It's all within us and could be so simple.
It was meant to be simple.
How can we get back to this place?

Be calm, be still, be quiet.

And you will learn so much about the world around you.

Just listen. The world will talk. The earth will talk.
Energy will talk.
Just *feel* and listen.

Plants

Wind feels to plants like stretching your muscles feels to humans.

Plants need to be loved like any other living species.

People admire plants for their beauty,
buy them and stick them in the ground,
and then neglect them.

Don't talk to them, don't listen to their needs, don't touch them—enough.

Plants need and want love and will tell you what they need and when they're happy, if you listen.

Free

Like a bird, I feel trapped when my freedom is gone.
Stuck in a cage where I can't sing my song.
Like a flower, I wilt when there's no sun or air.
My petals fall when conditions aren't fair.

I know what I need to grow—
It's freedom to dance, and to sing, and to fly with the wind.
I know what I need to blossom—
It's love that only I can give myself.

I hate feeling trapped more than anything in the world.

Kaleidoscope

Creativity, it seems, is beckoning me.
Restless and eager, I toss and turn.

Miles of visions,

        pages of thoughts,

wrestling to find their way

        out of my mind and into time,

where they can be displayed.

Polluted Mind

In my heart, I've always known I was a writer.
But, I guess I always questioned if I would be
good enough. As if I had to earn some merit
for the fulfillment I feel when my hand pushes ink
on a blank page, or when my fingers form patterns
to make words on a screen.
I remember the first time I decided to start writing my
book. I may have been 11 years old. I'd take a notebook
with me to the park and write about my life.

I'd write about how I'm 11 years old, but what I have to
say is still important—how I'm 11 years old, but I can feel
and think in ways that transcend any limits of time or age.
Sometimes, I wish I hadn't discouraged myself. So I could
look back and read what that mind had to offer—
before the pollution seeped in.

I See the World in You

Who am I to believe
in a world that is fair,
in a world that seeks justice,
kindness, and care?

Who am I to believe
that love still exists,
that it ever did,
that it's not a myth?

Who am I to believe
that a woman is strong,
more than an object
to just string along?

Who am I to believe
that there's power in thought,
that it's not all planned out,
that we haven't been bought?

Who am I to believe
there's a right way to do it,
to get to the top without cutting throats?
All of my peers seem so lost through it,
believing in lies that they call themselves.

It's not about heart,
it's about popularity,

an easy game to play with a single way out.

It's not about love,
it's about revenge,
playing for bodies to wrap their wounds.

It's not about brains,
cause those hardly exist,
replaced by computers we keep in our fists.

It's not about the world,
it's about ourselves,
the only thing that matters is how we're perceived.

But we're misled and misunderstood.
Everyone's in pain, they're just trying to hide it.
A smile here, a beer there, a day of sleep, a bag of weed.

It's a fun time, sure, but why do you need it?
Why's it so hard for you to put down?
Why's it so hard for us to look up,
gaze at the stars, and see ourselves?
Why's it so hard to pick up a book?
Flip through the pages, travel to Mars.
Why's it so hard to let people in,
to love and to cherish without endless sin?
Why's it so hard to look in the mirror,
naked and raw, and see yourself clearer?

Who am I to tell you that this is the way?
That there's right and there's wrong,

that you're choosing to stay—
Lost in the crowd, where you shouldn't have to fight for
a spot to be anything more than human—
More than divine.
Everyone wants to be more than just human—to have
power, to have thought, to fly.
But no one wants to accept being human,
accept that they are divine.
I see you looking at me, and I see myself too.
But how is that possible, looking at you?
Wake up.
Wake up.
Wake up.
And when you finally do,
realize that you were always me...and always YOU

The World

Burning Reflection

Who am I
lying on the bathroom floor—
tub overflowing,
wishing I could vomit some more?

My lack of emotion
confuses my soul,
while this mixture of potions
makes me feel whole.
Or does it? Who knows—
but I keep on drinking,
glasses still clinking,
my liver is sinking.

Eyes hazy and low
till my mind stops thinking.
I look in the corner
and see you winking.

I run with the feelings
I get in the moment—
still young, trying to live
with no signs of resentment.

My thoughts on this life
let me know I'm alive.
But I hate the feeling
of just floating by.

But how many can say
that they're serving a purpose?
I look 'round and see
my peers running a circus.
All lost and jumbled,
figuring out where to turn,
tripping and fumbling,
struggling to learn—

The importance of life
has a new connotation.
I hardly see hope
in my own generation.

A pretty face is all you need
to be so deceiving,
it's sad, but it's true—
all the lies you're believing.

My morals and truth
are still somewhat intact,
but it's hard when you see
what the world is enacting.

Showing the youth
there's no need for compassion,
so instead, they lash out
with all their aggression.

Love's just a word
that has lost all its worth,

and money's replaced it,
a brand-new birth.

But the look in your eyes
was all that I needed,
to see that my glory
had not been defeated.

I hope that in time,
this earth takes a turn,
for if not, we'll go down
as we watch the world burn.

A Breath at Dusk

To breathe doesn't mean you're alive.
What's a breath but a means to survive?

To feel doesn't make something real.
Your perception of life's just the peel.

Play in your mind for as long as you must.
Be careful your time doesn't turn into dust.

Dusk before dawn, it always repeats.
Searching for music to match my heart's beat.

Who am I now? It's an endless retreat
back into myself and off my feet.

The wave of the world's set just to compete.
But my presence is elsewhere, above the defeat.

Awake in this body, aware in this mind,
I'm holding the ticket you're aiming to find.

Stuck in the past, or lost in the future?
You're falling until you become your own suture.

Wait. Stop. Pause

Breathe in…
Now, breathe out.

Let yourself unwind, let go of all the doubt.

Become your own solution.
Ride your own wave.
Be rid of the pollution.
Never be a slave.

Questions to Consider

The things in life you can't explain
    come with thoughts of helpless pain.
    Sometimes, I think we're not meant to know.
    Is it best to just let go?

What does every day stand for?
    What can you and I do more?
    What's the point
    of life itself?
    Everyone's obsessed with wealth

Are you truly happy,
    on the inside?
    Pointing fingers at me,
    are you trying to hide?

Do you know the meaning of love?
    Can you understand?
    Do you believe in angels above,
    lending you a hand?

Why does every soul lie?
    Does it go that far?

Do you ever want to cry,
    but you just can't. make a tear?
    Have you ever had to say goodbye,
    as the one you love is about to die?

Is that your biggest fear?

Can you look into the mirror,
    and say you're proud of who you are,
    with a smile on your face?
    Or do you look into your own eyes,
    And wish you could erase?

Do you even care to know?
    Or are you going to just let go?

Decree to Be

I know I'm far from a queen,
but I need something to look up to
other than a dream.

Tell me, why does it seem
that everything is unobtainable?
Paying to survive,
this life is just so unexplainable.

And I myself am thriving
on the thought of something more.
I wake up every day and paint
a new world out my door.
Every step I take
is just a new way to explore
what's inside my very core,
'cause I refuse to lose this war—
refuse to give in.
Selling souls for a penny
is the world's biggest sin.

But we were built on lies,
even God is disguised,
so, how do we recognize
when love is right before our eyes?
The truth is we can't,
and if we can't even see,
then how can we be?

Pretty soon, being yourself
will be outlawed by the decree
that we must all be
the same—

Computers for a brain,
wires for a heart,
they'll label you insane
before they pick you apart.
That's how it always starts,
the oldest form of art:
destruction for creation
like a soul left to depart—
the only home it's ever known,
overthrown by a throne
made of cheap silicone.

I'd rather die alone
in my own little zone
than to become a clone
of another unknown.

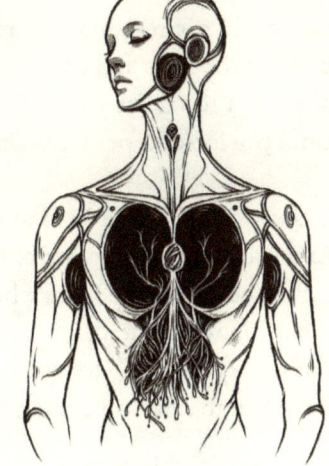

Far from a queen
but I had a dream
that gave me the key
to a world unseen.

Eternal Symphony

The thing about life
Is it keeps going…
No matter if you're ready or not.
No matter if you just need a second to breathe.
No matter if you ask nicely and say please.

Time. Will. Stop.
For no one.
Don't think that you are special.
You'll age, just like everybody else.

And one day,
You might not recognize yourself
Beneath the folds and cracks of your skin.
Might not recognize yourself
Until you look deeper than within.

One day, you'll find it hard to get up,
And realize your bones are brittle and get all fed up.
You'll remember the times when your body could do
What you wanted it to,
Without even having to try…
But when this day comes, don't cry.

Just remember what it took to get here,
Every breath your body took to bring you this far.
Remember all the lives you touched along the way,
And try to find peace in just being, this day.

Accept that you cannot beat time,
No matter how hard you try,
The cycle will always continue.
And the blip in time that is you
Will forever be remembered

As a note in this eternal symphony—
That is life.

Life's Mysteries

Close your eyes, and what do you see?
This life's the biggest mystery.

How can you tell the difference
between everything that's real?
How do you know perception
isn't judged by how you feel?

And every time you dream,
can you explain what you see?
Is it pure imagination?
Or is it life's secret key?

Is it hopes and all desires?
Is it fear that soon transpires?
Is it the real life you're in
until you wake up again?

I'll say we're all a little crazy,
and my days are often hazy,
but the insanity of my mind
is my most prized possession.
For a mind is one of a kind—
and mine you'll never find
'cause it's lost in this transgression.

So, just close your eyes, and what do you see?
This life's the biggest mystery.

Rambling Train

I need to reset my mind
or go back in time
to a train of simpler thought.
Where the thoughts on my brain
weren't money and pain,
but a new way that life could be taught.

See, all these material things
drive people insane,
and they don't even know they've been bought.
And money and fame
are all that remain,
everyone's just trying for a spot.

But what will you gain
standing up on that stage,
when inside you don't know who you are?
And all you can gain
is the praise of the world
'cause they all think that you are a star.

But what will you do
when you finally look back
and realize you've gone too far?
And there's no way to stop it
'cause inside your soul,
you're already waging a war.

See, that's all I see
when I look around—
people out of place.
They all look lost,
but they're hiding it well
while they're looking for a space—

A space where they fit
and won't have to hide
the shame that's on their face.
A space where they feel
they can finally be free,
free without a trace—

A trace of what was,
a trace of what is,
and a trace of what might ever be.

Some hope that the world's
not as dark as it seems
and that there'll be a light they can see.
But the light that they seek
is only within,
and the only way in is to be.

Only then will you flee
false reality
and gain your victory.

Who's Driving?

Passenger to my mind, I can't tell you who's driving.
Sometimes, I'm autopilot, other times, I'm just surviving
in a world of my own,
hidden in a clone of another unknown.

To think I'm alive as just a cell of the world,
only living in time, like a blink of an eye.
My mind is a seed struggling to grow,
confined by these laws and these bones I don't know.

Where do I go, when nowhere is home?
'Cause I'm stuck in a world where love is not shown,
but hate is rewarded for those who condone.
It's like heaven is sealed, and hell has the throne,
but maybe our balance is just overthrown.

Hand me my wings, I can't seem to reach.
And give me the strength that I need to teach.
Help me instill truth in the minds
of those who are willing to listen to mine.

Unbind my soul, it's been trapped for too long,
I'm starting to wonder to whom it belongs,
'cause the taste in my mouth is just a bit bitter,
but I can't give up, no, I won't be a quitter.

Not to the game, nor to the fame
It's the only way out, they'll remember my name.

Say I'm insane 'cause I swallowed their pain,
but for me, it's a gain,
and they won't take the blame.

Take a quick bite, reach for the hook,
but be careful not to overlook.
Open your mind, I just want a look.
Now tell me, who's driving—you or a crook?

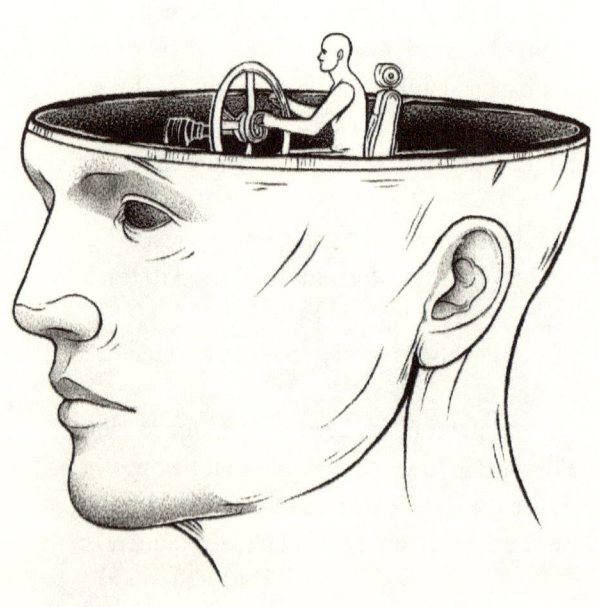

Pretty Privilege

How far down does the sun go, I wonder.
What's on the other side?
One sunset is one sunrise,
And I'm lost looking into your eyes.

Do you really see me?
Or do you see the vessel I inhabit?
Curly brown hair and golden-brown eyes,
But what's on the inside?

Would you want me lying next to you
If I didn't have this frame?
Would you still want to make love to me
Even if I were insane?

Am I forgiven more easily
Because of this sweet smile?
Treated much nicer,
Despite all things vile.

I want to know I'm loved
For the ugliest of moments.

If my face possessed no beauty
Would I be put on the streets?
Thrown away so raggedly,
How many hearts beat?

I see you, sweet soul,
Stop looking at your feet.
Hold your head up high,
Even when you feel defeat.

L.A. Water

There's something in the water,
that makes you vain and shallow,
and everything is about
me, ME, **ME!**

Stop Comparing

Comparison is the strongest poison,
subconsciously, you're dead,
keeping up with them and everyone
you deem to be ahead.

What's the timeline? What's the rush?
Are you happy as you are?
Life is fake if all you're doing is wishing from afar.

Don't believe all the media.
Don't believe all the smiles.
Don't believe that all your peers
are ahead of you by miles.

This life's a game, it always has been,
just keep your eyes and ears alert.
Watch your back and push forward
or else you're bound to end up hurt.

Put your energy into you.
You're the only thing that's worth it.
Let the pieces fall into place,
And know that you deserve it.

Gramercy

I looked at this city once and saw an oyster—
lights spread out for miles.
A quilted city,
just to warm her dreams.
Those dreams,
so close to reality,
it pained her not to be living
in her accepted truth.
This city is beautiful
no matter what rooftop you're on.
From the tops of elder buildings,
everything seems much more clear.
You're away from screams of ragged souls
who beg for you to hear—
Their pain.
Their rage.
Their story.
Do they recognize themselves when they look
in the mirror?
It's crazy what a city does to your hopes and dreams.
I think of what it took to bring this city fame,
and erase with it the fortitude for minds to stay sane.
From the rooftops of Los Ángeles
I am here to ease your brain.
Let your burdens loose,
scream again, again, again.

The Shape of Humans

Tell me—
Is this how it's supposed to be?
What life is all about?
A bunch of wandering faces
trying to figure it all out?

When I was younger,
I had hopes and dreams beyond compare.
But as I grow with age,
I'm wondering if what's left is just despair.

Those things that once seemed full of life
and endless possibility,
were struck by truth and hidden lies
that hindered my mobility—
to be and do and conquer
all the quests that I had dreamt.
Now, all I'm doing is wondering
what it even meant.

I'm better than I was,
but worse than how I want to be.
Older and wiser,
but further from the real me.

These shapeless humans hold the key
to life's purest destruction.
A loss of self, though unintended,

feeds into obliteration.

I can't connect the way I wish
with any other soul.
There is no meaning in my acts
that others feel consoled by.
I wish I could just hold on to
the part of me that's true,
the part that has enough to give
to both myself and you.

Yet sadly, I do not know
if that part will ever surface.
It's buried under secrets
that the universe effaced.

I'm holding on to all I know—
I cannot be abolished.
Within me is an unknown breed,
and in time, our seeds will flourish.

COVID-19

They say the end is near,
try to flood our minds with fear,
no job, no sun, all distance,
makes for quite the newest year.

On the corners of the street, they whisper
Martial law—
The rise of the apocalypse,
the beginning of the fall.

There are men lined up for guns,
people coughing in the street,
there's no bread, no eggs, no water,
and there's dirt on your feet.

Toilet paper is being hoarded,
streets are being boarded,
there's no planes to get here or there,
and the youth just doesn't care.

Maybe it's just comedy,
a way to ease the pain,
give them some relief
for the anxiety in their brain.

Everyone's saying it's weird,
now that they can see
the world for what it's been—

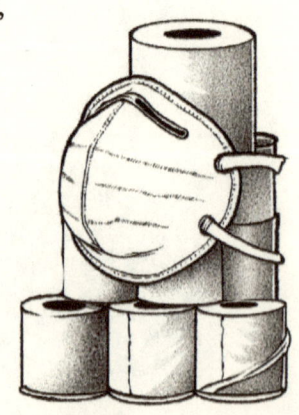

112

I tried to tell you what would be.

In the grasp of a virus
the only thing that's clear
is that humanity is inhumane;
the majority, insane.
For us to feel normal
someone has to feel pain.
Built with soft petals,
trained to be a machine,
pushing and pushing
working under the crown
till we wear ourselves down—
because we're so tough.
We have to be useful,
or we're not enough.

Learn to exist, to cease, to breathe,
It's okay to just be, let it be, feel free.

Do the trees and the wind and the sea cry to be?
Stress themselves out till there's nothing to see?
No.
They just be. They just are. They're just free—
Something that's lost in humanity.

Where is God?

Are we forsaken on this plane?
For your presence hardly remains.
I search for you in day-to-day
but find only shadows cast away.
Your name no longer heard in passing,
giggles passed at you when asking
Where is God?

Does God exist in present day?
I say, "Yes, of course, please pray."
There's not a moment that has passed
without God who forever lasts
Inside of us.

But I see beggars on the street,
people left to eat
nothing but dirt
from on their feet,

It sickens me.

I see children with no knowledge of a God,
with no morals to uphold within their bod.

I see hate, and lust, and envy
guiding a generation left to ending—
what it means to be an angel in this world.

I see the galaxies are moving away
from little Earth,
causing questions as to what we are worth.
Will there be another birth?
Will there be another chance?
Or are we forsaken on this planet?
Will this be our final dance?

Lost in the abyss that is true.

What Decade is it Now?

In a world that's constantly changing, I can't keep up.
I thought I was adaptable, but *what the fuck*?

**I grew up in a world where we played outside, and
our imagination could take any day to new heights.**
Now, every 3-year-old has a phone and knows how to use
it.

**I grew up in a world where tigers and polar bears
lived.**
Now, all the exotic animals are going extinct,
while aquariums and zoos are becoming
digital experiences.

**I grew up in a world where rap was rhythm and
poetry.**
Now, it's repeating the same thing over and over and over
again, and thinking that it's worthy of a title.

**I grew up in a world where handwritten letters were
cute.**
Now, no one even knows what a stamp is,
and social media rules the earth.

**I grew up in a world where degrees were respected
and worth the money it took to get them.**
Now, everyone has a degree, no one's making money,
and the world is drowning in debt.

I grew up in a world where information came from books.
Now, it comes from the click of a finger
and can't even be trusted.

Triggered by a Hair

I'm way more privileged than I realized.
And it took a hair in my water for me to see
that I need to humble myself,
been misdirecting my wealth.
I'm sitting cozy in my bed
while infants are losing their heads—
This is America.
I should be glad that I'm free.
But I'm ashamed to call myself part of something you see
that stands for nothing.
We don't have an agenda;
we're just the biggest hypocrites in town.
It's all propaganda,
there is no bravery.
There are no ethics to this shit.
It's give me, give me more,
don't matter what it takes to get.

I met a young man on a yacht;
he said to me one day,
"No one gets anywhere by playing fair."
"They won't remember your name."
That hit me hard.
And even though I don't believe it
there's a trillion fucking stories
that'll prove it, you can see it.

We're just reckless.

I'll step on you to get to who?
Someone bigger and better,
and then I'll stab them too?

What is this game?
I'll pay you to follow me
just to seem like I have clout.
Nah, that's a mess,
don't bother me, I'm out.

Why does it matter?
Take away your pretty phone,
now show me who you are—
Under the filters, skin to bone,
you're just like me.
You laugh and cry and shit.
And that's all it takes to be a person
but you'll probably forget
'cause you have "fans."
But will they follow you to death?
Will they be right by your side
when you're suddenly a no-one, changing tide?
I bet they won't.
But then again, who will?
What's it even mean to be a friend?
I hardly talk to mine, and still
I say I love them,
and that's an even bigger story.
But the lie built on America
is the reason we have glory.

Now, please sit down.
And then be grateful you're alive.
It means you have a fighting chance,
this revolution will survive,
I say amen!

The Abyss

A brush of cold air gives me pleasure,
but the burning inside of me takes it away.
The thoughts of the past— they still linger
as I'm held by the arms, the ghosts of yesterday.

Somehow, it's never enough.
What you do has been done,
what you say has been said.
And you say I'm just too tough.
But the fact is I'm reading a story I've read—

Again and again, it's the same.
It's hard to go on when you know the ending.
And even when I turn the page,
I keep hoping this time that you'll pick your own lane.

But when will it ever be different?
You give them free will, and they all act the same,
then beg you to SEE that they're different.
And when you refute, it's your name that they blame.

Tell me, what kind of prison is hell?
And when you describe it, then answer me this…
Is that not how we're living as well?
Surrounded by darkness but living in bliss.

You're bothered when my face is hollow,
but claim that you want me to be genuine.

And sometimes what I say's hard to swallow,
but still, you're fighting a way to get in—

Again and again, it's the same.
It's hard to go on when you know the ending.
And even when I turn the page,
I keep hoping this time that you'll pick your own lane.

And I know that I can change it
by not turning the page and just walking away.
But part of me wants to face it,
indulge in the truth by choosing to stay.

But how do I make them SEE
that this world is insanity?

Seems the only way I can stay afloat
is by swimming in the abyss,
but when I go diving, somehow,
there's always someplace that I'm missed.

Of my own mind,
in my own time,
I'm lost in the abyss.
But what's keeping me here
are these memories of bliss.

Heartless & Soulful

Past, present, and preparation.
You can't get lost if there's no destination.
Life's just a game, or maybe it's not,
but I do guarantee it's not what you thought.

Two decades I've been on this earth,
but I've known I was different ever since birth.
Trying to offset the balance, change the way things turn,
introduce a new dance, give you something to learn.

Heartless and soulful at the same damn time,
does that mean soul and body aren't intertwined?
I ask myself questions, but nobody can answer,
just like I ask myself why nobody's cured cancer.

Seems nobody's really focused on those kinds of things,
everybody's too caught up in all those 'finer' things.
Spending money like they got it when it doesn't exist,
then they're wondering what happened with their empty
fists.

Strangers sleeping in your bed, but it's fine by you,
'cause the sex eases your head, and it's something to do.
Everybody has their vice; baby, tell me what's yours?
I'm just trying to be enticed by you opening your doors.

I keep questioning this journey, wondering if it ever ends,
I'm sitting in reality, while everybody else pretends.

But I'll tell you in time, just remember my name,
I'm far from my prime, but I'm bound to inflame.

City of Angels

Feeling like I'm being stripped down to my bone
in this city that I've always heard so much about.
Wanted something new, somewhere to call my home,
but I quickly realized that eventually I'm getting out.

See, the glamour and glitz that we're shown on TV
are really nothing but shits wiped along all the streets.
Yeah, the Hollywood stars, they ain't much to see,
just another sidewalk if you fucking ask me.

And most of the real stars are beat the fuck up,
'cause this city is cold, it'll eat you right up.
And yet, here I am, chasing a dream.
Hoping it becomes fruitful before I become mean.

You either make it or break it,
it takes one shot.
And if somehow you can't keep up,
better hope you don't get got.

But I won't sell my soul
for a chance of fleeting fame,
I'd rather keep all my character
and hold all this pain,
stay true to my name,
say fuck all the games.
You're either with me, or you're not—
I couldn't care either way.

In The City of Angels,
I wonder where they sleep.
'Cause I've yet to see one,
haven't even heard a peep.
But I've taken my leap,
still somewhere in the air,
hoping I land on my feet.

I'm still alive,
and I guess that means I'm soaring.
Guess they gave me hidden wings
to help me pull these magic strings—
so now it's pedal to the metal,
and I'm flooring.

Just don't forget to look up,
don't forget to slow down,
and when all is said and done
remember what it took to get your crown.

Porcelain Skin

As I pluck these tiny hairs
from my soft brown skin,
I'm reminded of the perfect woman,
made of porcelain.

Not a hair found anywhere
except upon her head,
such a shame it'd be to see the truth,
the man is so misled.

Misled into a trap
that only he creates,
envisioning the perfect woman
in his mind, where he escapes.

She waits for him there peacefully,
she hardly makes a noise.
For the perfect woman has no voice
unless it's one the man enjoys.

Silent, smooth, and poised.
The image mustn't be destroyed.
The perfect woman lies awaiting
just to be deployed—

Solely to stimulate
the man who aims to dominate
until he penetrates

Deep into her core.

He'll always ask for more.
Until the perfect woman's worn,
then she's out the door
until he finds another,
better than before.
The perfect woman once again
hung up like plush décor.

Made to be adored,
waiting to be explored,
the perfect woman patient
as she's patently ignored.

The man returns to find his
perfect woman on the floor.
Cracked porcelain eyes and limbs,
free from bounded porcelain skin.

Finally awakened.
The perfect woman is no more.

Entangled with Life

I think I'm learning what it means to just be.
Within my own element, there's peace.
Think I'm truly understanding what it means to be free
without chaos and sadness ruling me.

Almost 30 years have gone by
since I first opened my eyes
to the crippling world surrounding me,
not a clue what it would come to be.

So toxic, it seeped inside my pores,
muddying my spirit, siphoning my core.
Filled with passion, I always hoped for more
than this entanglement with life that felt like war.

But now I see the truth,
see the blessing that is youth,
see the choices that I've made,
that have led me to today.

Now, I see the beauty in acceptance
and in letting go.
And rejoice in what it means
to exist inside this ebb and flow.

Engaging in this vain and baneful plane
of existence, nearly drove me insane.

Feeling the life within me drained,
just hoping someone would remember my name.

From my roots, I know that I'm pure.
Even if it seems like I'm not.

And to keep out the monsters and harden my shell,
I adapted, becoming parallel—

To all of that around me.
So well, it made me sick.
Looking in the mirror, it never seemed to click—

How could I be so pure?

Calling angels to do good feats
while I'm tiptoeing over deceit
just to keep myself from defeat,
making sure I don't deplete.

So tender, I locked myself away.
Forgetting that love's the only way.
I dusted myself in sin to say
I'm not holy, because neither are they.

Plucked my wings to fit in,
it kept the pressure off my back.
But it only ended up being an attack

On my own soul—
Restless and eager
to feel whole
again.

Adam and Eve

Who knew that Adam would lie?
It would all become clear after things went awry.
Ashamed of his lack of self-control,
he threw Eve into the flame and switched her role.

It's been told millions of times,
stuffed down the throat of feeble minds,
that women are the sin.
Evil temptresses akin—
to Adam.

But never his equal.
Only the pain on his hip,
taken from his rib.
Oh, get a grip!

(Can't tell me you really believe that shit.)

I seldom speak the truth
in a world such as this—
It falls easily down the drain.
Either dismissed
or laughed at.
Causing outrage in some
who believe it is *his* domain.
But let me explain…

You say women are the helpers, but who's helping who?
You give me your seed; I sow and brew.
I bring forth the life, bring forth the new.
(What is it again you do?)

While I'm with child, who's fetching me food,
keeping me warm, trying to subdue?
When anger gets the best of you,
who's there to calm and nurture you?

Whose body possesses power that makes others weak?
Brings a man to his knees, makes him fight through defeat.
Whose good graces must a man be on,
to be invited *in*—
to a world so warm, you had to call it sin…?

How could something feel so good
if it wasn't rooted in evil?
Women to be controlled so a man won't lose his head.
It's clear to see the story told,
and why most of the world's misled.

Every month I shed, I rebuild myself again.
And when I have conceived, I make milk from within—
My breasts.
Push out a human from below my waist,
and heal myself again.

What is it you do? Does your body do that, too?
No intention to offend, but you must see the truth.

In nature, who we call "Mother,"
males have their mates but often get eaten after the deed
is done.
Give me your seed.
There's no longer need,
for you.

In humans, the need is to protect and to help,
to provide seed and shelter.

Creation and nurturing build the people and the land.
Protectors will always be helpers.

Both are needed.
But do not get confused with who is and has always been
in control
behind the scenes.
The only control you have
is that which you've stolen.
That which you take—when you rape—
because you feel so *out* of control...

Men have been bred for violence,
women for love.
Let's not tip the scale.

Women, while fierce and capable of violence
will lose power if violence is abused.

Dancing Through Flames

Tip toe, tip toe,
Why must we go so slow?
Dance around the flames until they slowly lose their glow.
We're thrown into the fire but swear we don't feel pain,
Just to show the image that we're able to maintain—
Able to abstain
From that which makes us human.
Like humanity's a crime,
And a feeling is a nuisance.
Who made these laws?
And who gave them the applause
To make them transform every act of love into a flaw?

Emotion is a weakness,
And a gun in hand is strength,
And somehow murdering souls
Is just the perfect length,
To show that we're the fearless, the baddest
and the strong,
without even a question in the mind whether it's wrong.

Desensitize the youth.
Demoralize the schools.
And teach them that the only form of praise is in the rules.

When did compassion become shame?
When did love become a game?
And when did the politicians in the race become insane?

We can't be guided as a country by fools in precious ties.
We have to learn to guide ourselves and quickly realize—

Tick tock, tick tock,
Time is running out.
Dance around the truth until it finally comes out.

Escaping all the lies might be the hardest thing to do.
But somewhere in your eyes lies the start of something
new.

Breaks and Love Begins

Untended Wounds

You had untended wounds that got messy—

You were bleeding on me,
and every time you dripped blood,
it was someone else's name.

Have Heart

All these emotions got me floatin'
in a sea of self-pity.
Although I'm coastin', always toastin',
in my mind, I can't agree
with who I was, and who I am,
and who I'm still trying to be,
and everyone on the outside has no idea I'm lonely.

Lonely.
Lonely…
The word itself's a melody,
rolling off the tongue, it hits your soul and sinks in deep.

If you only knew the pain inside of me
maybe then you'd understand why I always smile,
for you, not me.

It hurts to cry.
'Cause every time I do
I'm reminded of the tears that fought to
hide themselves from you.
The one who brought me in this world,
you took me away too,
'cause I hid from who I was out of fear just to please you.
Perfection was never perfect,
I could never compete
with the life you had planned out for me,
I was born into defeat.

From a father who never wanted me,
how could I ever succeed?
In your eyes, I was the reason for your burden,
so you took it out on me.

But was it worth it?
Yes, in fact, you made me strong,
but the love that you missed out on
would have never done you wrong.
I am your daughter, and I'll love you through it all,
even if you never call,
'cause I know no one can be perfect
and every now and then, we fall.

And I have fallen.
But I've recognized my strength,
my ability to get back up supersedes all of my angst.
And I will rise, and show the world just who I am.
With every song and every action—
trust in me, I've got a plan.

I'm an artist at heart,
that's why I always fall apart,
but I exist in this world
to remind you to have heart.

Songs From a Dove

It wouldn't be wise to fall in love,
'cause little boy, I'm just a dove.
A dove who'll spread its wings and fly,
and leave you there alone to cry.

Though many have gazed upon my wings
and wished for me to stay,
none have heard the song that sings,
for I've always flown away.

So little boy, don't get too close,
just look from where you are.
'Cause that's the closest you can get
to a dove who's like a star.

And little boy, don't get too close,
don't try to clip my wings.
For I'm a dove that's meant to fly,
the dove whose soul can never die.
For I'm the dove that no one knows,
the dove that comes but always goes.

Cessation of Desire

Rain to drown the pain
makes it hard to hear my sorrows.
Sleeping through the days
leaves behind unseen tomorrows.

To feel you on my skin used to somehow be enough.
But all of that has faltered,
seems it's just become too tough—
to deal with the feelings
that you say won't go away,
your heart fixed on a memory
waiting endlessly at bay.

But holding on to nothing
is the surest way to drown,
while hoping just for something
makes it easy to break down.
Though passion still exists,
its enemy grows stronger,
and pain itself insists
not to persist any longer.

Lost hearts caught in a web,
spun from carelessness and yen,
fight only just for freedom
and amity within.
But to save what has been lost
is to burn inside a fire,

and the only way out is
the cessation of desire.

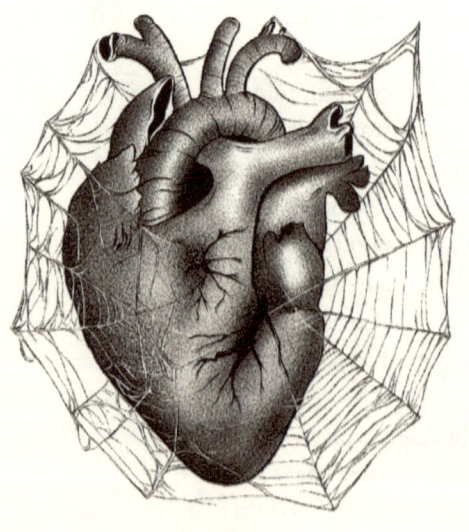

Forever's Lost Inside of You

I'm at home when I'm alone.
It's the saddest, truest lie.
It's a lonely contradiction
forever making me ask, *why?*

Why my being is like poison, to those who have a taste.
Why it seems they can't let go,
won't let a second go to waste.
Claiming that I "aim to hurt them,"
that I'm "dangerous" and "bad."
Yet they don't want to let go,
like I'm the best they've ever had.
But they know that isn't true.
Baby boy, look at you,
getting all mixed up and jumbled,
like you haven't got a clue.

Trust me, I don't want to hurt you,
it's not my goal when I wake up.
But baby, I don't want to love you,
so please just back the fuck up.

It's not that I don't care about you, but I'm numb to it all,
the shit that I've been through makes it impossible to fall.

'Cause I'm always on my guard,
I think I'm locked inside forever.

145

The funny part about it all is that I once believed forever
was an endless place for love, a place that couldn't die.
But forever's just a memory, or maybe just a lie.

But wherever forever went, is where my heart went too,
it's locked inside forever, forever's lost inside of you.

A Libra

Some people say it pains them to be alone.
Well, I say those who are alone are more prone to being grown,
harder like a stone, almost always unknown.

Wandering eyes are common, but so are wandering hands,
and wandering thoughts can't help but wonder
what it's like on unknown lands.

She quickly glances over; both of your eyes meet.
Now the only thing that's keeping you at a distance is your feet.
But hers are moving towards you, and you don't want to leave;
everything she aims to give you, you're willing to receive.

But to receive is to deceive,
now perceive who is deceived—
the one longing to achieve... or the one left to grieve?
Or the one who is naïve, left only to conceive—

Truth for what it is, more for what it's not.
Another in the picture wasn't even in her thought.

She pulls you close and kisses you;
you linger on her breath.
Now, this beginning starts to unravel a new death.

Loyalty and lies, how can they coexist?
One within the other adds a kinky little twist.
But tell me, what's the point
when you're playing two roles?
Both beside each other only messes up your goals.

Some people say it pains them to be alone,
but I can't imagine any other person on this throne.
With all I've been shown, I would rather be alone
than be in the arms of another unknown.

The Cycle of the Wound

I was born knowing life,
I was born with understanding,
but somehow, all I know and feel has made me
so demanding.

I want too much out of life—
or do I just want what's enough?
I don't know, but either way, somehow,
I've ended up so tough.

I wanted love long ago, I wanted never to let go,
but now I'm left feeling okay if I end up all alone.

You say it's love that you show, I say it's what you don't
know
that keeps your fire burning for me, even through the
snow.

You say to just accept it, but baby, if you only knew
there's no room here in this soul of mine for even part of
you.

I'd rather go through hell all on my own, searching for
what's true,
than ever bring someone along or hear them say the words
"I do."

'Cause I do will fade away and somehow turn into I can't,
and then we're left with all these wishes that we know we'll
never grant.

It's always fun for a while, until it all kicks in,
and then you're left wondering how you're even
in the mess you're in.

But I guess it's all life, right? We're born straight into sin.
And we'll keep living again until we finally win.

But what happens if we do? Do we finally ascend?
Or do we stay right where we are until the wounds of
Earth mend?

I don't know, but ask yourself, are you where you want to
be?
And if not, then find a way to finally set yourself free.

150

Thorns & Roses

Thorns and roses, thorns and roses,
they exist within each other.
You can have a bad day, but tomorrow brings another.
And yes, it's hard to find good in this world full of bad,
but even when you're moving forward,
remember what you had.
'Cause when you're picking up roses, remember to feel
all the scars from the thorns that still ache just to heal.
There's pain, and there's sadness, but without their every beat,
it would make all the good seem a little less sweet.

Thorns and roses, thorns and roses,
every flower has a flaw,
and even yet and still, somehow, you're left in awe.
Fighting battles, pointing fingers,
but where does that get us?
With all the love we have, tell me why we always fuss.
Hardened hearts and broken feelings,
but still, we seem to stay.
'Cause somehow what we feel seems to always outweigh.

You can pick up a rose, but without its precious thorn,
it's simply a flower, mistakably torn.

151

Baby, it's Yes, or it's No

Late nights, cold fights,
hot breath against air.
Pushed up against a wall,
her only weapon is her stare.
And the scream she lets out
rattles tears from her eyes,
the call from her lungs
makes her anger arise.

Hands gripped on the wheel,
but her vision is blurred,
and the light from the moon
shines the only path to a destination.
If covered by a cloud,
say hello to pure damnation.

Pain eaten off a skewer,
poison sipped from a spoon,
like shit was hand made from a brewer,
this life was soaked in too soon.
And she sits in contemplation
of the earth and its rotation,
knowing karma is a bitch,
so keep me out of circulation.

Shattered glass on the floor,
scattered red against the walls,
dripping like her veins,

unanswered like her calls.
And her shadow is a cloud of smoke
that tethers at her heel.
Burns when sliding down her throat
like an electric eel.

The smoke and alcohol she swallows
takes away the feel,
and puts her in a state of trance
to take away what's real.

She quietly undermines the fact that
everything ain't what it seems.
Getting caught up in the wrong
and losing sense in helpless dreams.

Stricken by your words,
but stabbed by your eyes.
Love flown away like birds,
heart forcefully defies.

Fading consciousness and sanity,
short breaths begin to fire.
Heightened anxiousness, anxiety—
force the soul through body to transpire.

Black suns jailed in her iris,
widening with distress,
the darkness in her mind
pushes deeply to molest.

Limp body shaken in a room,
sprawled out across your bed.
What is anybody to assume
when the image is misled?
And the truth is left unsaid?
But baby, maybe all you needed
was a deadbolt and a shed.

Jumper cable to the heart
to revive what I have lost.
Fleeting feelings in a dart
aimed at yours to soon defrost…
'Cause your hardened chest is frozen,
but it's not the only one.
So tell me with a love like this one,
how is one to feel the sun?

Take a flame to the ice,
let it melt in your hand,
if what's left is enough
what's inside will expand.

Can you see what I say?
Can you hear what I show?
Can you feel what's real?
Baby, it's yes, or it's no.

Unforgiving Dream

Everything, everything, everything, everything
Is a dream, dream, dream, dream, dream.
Everything, everything, everything, everything
Is a dream, it's all a dream...

To me, it seems that I can't be everything I wanted to.
With you, it seems that I can't love the way I felt I could.
But it's all in my head, unforgivable mess,
it's true, I bleed like you.

Nothing more, nothing less,
rest my head on your chest,
hear the sounds of 1,000 storms.

Let me in, I ask oh so frequently,
let me see you're unveiled soul,
pure vulnerability.

You have every right to be weary with that soul,
and I deserve a fight, but my love, it's shivering, cold.
And all alone, I wish that I could simply hold...
On
to something.
On
to someone
new was never what I needed,
you could never be defeated.

I just get so worried that it's never good enough,
always trying to call your bluff.
It's a shame it always beats this way
when inside, it's all a dream.

Lost

Lost in this dream that is you and I,
wondering how, when, and simply why,
locking your eyes, trying to let you in,
letting you know I'm confused.

My heart's always fluttered and faded the same,
my mind quickly wanders, darts off on a game,
I've always been quicker and harder to tame
than most.

It's hindering me,
not letting me see
more than potential for just you and me.
I'm losing my interest, "It's not you, it's me."
Lost in a mess of my own.

Simplicity, so simple.
Monogamy, so plain.
It pains me to think I'm alone.

Can't you see I'm trying?

The honey's lost its sweet,
it's hard for me to meet
you there.

Sometimes it's hard for me to care,
but I always do.

157

That's how I know I love you.
Or maybe I think I do.
Or maybe I'm confused.
What's new?

I'll Share a Song

How did you teach my arms to fill the empty spaces?
How did you teach my heart to not feel all the rain?
I took a chance with you against my better judgment.
I didn't listen to the tick inside my brain.

Now I'm aching, aching, reaching for the moon,
Hoping that I see a glimpse inside my room.
Aching, aching
You don't even know this,
Don't even notice…

All of the nights you keep me up, I'm always waiting.
All of the times I wish you'd stop and just see me.
I shouldn't have to ask for your appreciation,
I shouldn't feel in need in times when you are there.

But I'm aching, aching, reaching for the moon,
Hoping that I see a glimpse inside my room.
Aching, aching, you don't even know this,
Don't even notice.

You've got a heart without a home,
And I tried to give you somewhere to roam.
You'll let me fade right into you
But I can't let go, 'cause I know, you're a fool.
'Cause you don't know this,
Don't even notice.

I hope you remember the first song that I wrote you,
And all of the times that I shared while you faded
into sleep,
You let me mutter my peep.

Aching, aching
Just another me
Wanting to love
Just another you.

Broken

Any open invitation
she takes without hesitation,
filling that empty void,
such desperation.

Broken up, broken down,
four years spent searching for the crown
that never left her head.
Unwavered, and undead.

Biting lips beside her bed,
heartbeat inside her head,
the sound repeats.

Pinch from below her waist,
life sucked and thrown like waste,
tears hidden from her face,
she's gone.

Child mother to child.
A mother can't forget.
My baby, don't forget
my love.

I love you still,
in my arms.
Forgive me.
For I never knew love until you,

never knew love could burn blue,
always thought I would choose you,
it's true.

Broken up, broken down,
I'm shattered glass lying on the ground
saying, *don't get cut.*

The Cold

Never thought I'd be so cold, so old.
Never thought I'd have to kill another soul.
Never thought I'd leave you there to unfold,
unravel yourself, show your softest gold.

I used to be the one whose heart could never falter,
the one whose firm convictions no one could ever alter.
I used to be the one who was able to console,
let you leave all your secrets with me, still untold.

I've always been bold, but I've never been cold,
feels like somehow I'm filling this mold,
leaving my insides, fit to be sold,
there'll be little left for anyone to hold.

I look at how easy it is to not beat,
to not feel a pulse, not even feel my feet.
I look in the mirror and see the deceit;
it's like staring at someone you know you can't meet.

Who is she? So far from me, I can't see what she could be,
but she knows you, and you know her; she claims to be
me.

Behold, never thought I'd be so cold, so young.
Never thought I'd let you hear the whispers from my
tongue.
Never thought you'd end up clung, so sprung,

pulled a dagger from your chest,
now you're left to be hung.

I'll always be the one whose heart can never falter,
the one whose firm convictions no one will ever alter.
But the image in your head I can never uphold,
though the secrets in my bed will remain untold.

Never thought I'd be so cold, so young.
Never thought I'd hear my songs be sung.
Never thought I'd ever see *the one*
to melt my solid heart— my golden Sun.

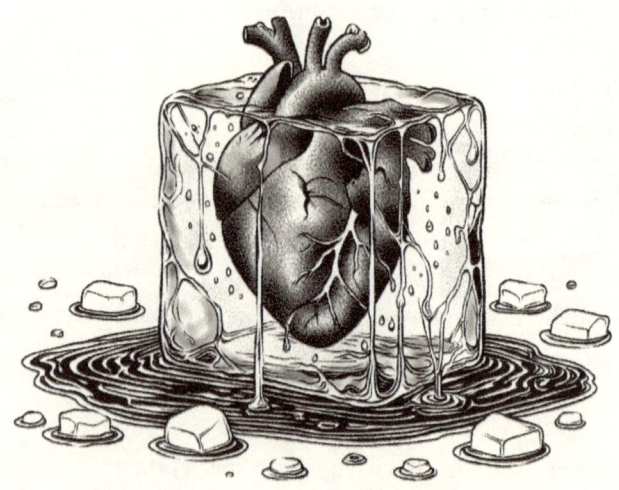

Will You Love Me?

Underneath all of my flesh,
If my skin begins to rot and fall
and bones are all that's left,
Will you love me?

When my smiles turn to frowns,
And I let you in to see all of the things keeping me down,
Would you love me?

If you never saw my eyes…and I never made you laugh,
Would you love me without all I've done to show you who
I am?

Without all your false perceptions,
Without all my perfect imperfections,

Could you love me if I were just me?
My soul alone, eternally,
Could you love me?

Or do you just love what you see?
Everything that's on the surface, everything that isn't me,
Can you love me?

When I show you who I am,
When I'm no longer sweet or pretty,
Will you see all that I am?

I am not what I look like,
I am not what I seem,
I want you to look through me,
And tell me what you see,

Do you love me?

Love and Company

I want you.
More than words can express,
but I'm so scared to lose you,
I'm just such a mess.

I long for you, and I want you to stay.
As much as I push
I can't have you away.

I want you to see that I'm trying to love you,
love you in ways you're not used to.
Love you and hold you and be in your arms,
I know you can't tell, but I'm just so afraid that you'll go.

People always go.
They're scared to be loved even when they want it the
most.
They're scared of the pain and the hurt and the loss,
so they dream in their minds,
but it's never as good as they hope.

I look at you and want to pull you close to me,
but I fear that you won't feel my love.
I know I can be suffocating, and I've vowed never to be
that way again,
So, I love from a distance.

You'd never know that I'm aching for you

just to love me back
harder.
And harder.
Come here.

I want to be cute and stupid in love where we can't keep
our hands off each other.
Where we miss each other, even if it's only been a few
minutes.
I want to be comfortable enough to fall and trust that
you'll be right there with me.
I give you so much space because I don't want to drown
you in me...
I don't want to love you so hard that you run... away...
from... me.
But in this space, I'm constantly longing.

People think they want love until they get it
and then realize—they just want company.

The Saga

I'd be lying if I said I didn't want you in my bed,
can't get you out of my head,
I hate you leaving me on read.
Can't help but think that I might've just fucked up,
looking past the clues, refused to let them all add up.

I guess I should've known this window
wouldn't last forever,
opportunities come and go,
just like this (ever-changing) weather.
I can't help but be a fool to think you'd see me in a light
brighter than the girl you were with the other night.

But just wait, stop, pause,
is that really what you want?
To rewrite the same old book,
this time in a different font?

'Cause I can tell you how it ends
if you really wanna know...
She'll love you just enough until she's ready to let go
again. But I get it— it's something you already know,
you just wanna feel loved, and you don't wanna tell her
no.

But I can promise if you let me
I'll be better than the rest,
never let you feel like you were ever second best.

I know I hide my feelings well,
nobody ever could tell
I was steady waiting on a clue
until you rang the bell.

And even still, I had a doubt,
too scared to see just what about,
but now I wish I had taken the bait,
you laid it all out.

So don't go, don't go,
don't let it be too late.
I refuse to let this be
the hidden road blocked off by fate.

Angel Eyes

Angel eyes that haunt me even though I'm far away,
with you or without you, I can't seem to be okay.

Wrapped inside confusion,
sprinkling self-doubt on my meals,
I've quickly gone from in control to always in my feels.

Cascading waves of horror on a loop inside my mind,
my dreams are getting darker,
meaning's getting hard to find.

I'm angry, then I'm laughing, and I know I'm losing touch,
reality keeps slipping past, living's just become too much.

I love you, but I hate you too,
especially if you care.
'Cause then I might believe you too,
and that just isn't fair.

And if I were to die today
there'll be nothing in your arms
to let you know that I'm okay
and safe away from harm.

I love you, but I hate you too,
especially if you care.
'Cause then I might believe you too,
and that just isn't fair.

Neither to me, nor to you.
In the end, it's always blue.

Lesson on love

You're walking down the street, along a trail, or wherever
you may be, and a flower catches your attention.
It's so beautiful that you can't help but stare at it and wish
it to be yours. You think about plucking it from its stem
or cutting it from its roots to bring it home with you,
but what will happen to your flower once you do?

Chances are, the second you remove it from its habitat, it
will slowly begin to die. And even if you can care for it,
it won't be the same. Your flower will no longer be the
same.

The best way to love and admire it is to do so in a way that
won't change the flower or take away its freedom and life.
Leave the flower where it is, and every day you pass by, it
will be as beautiful as ever. It will blossom just for you.
Learn to love it by allowing it to be.

Instead of cutting it from its roots to hog its beauty, let it
be free and let others admire its beauty as well.

I say this in hopes I can save a flower from misguided
admiration. For I, too, was once a flower... a bird...
someone, somewhere else, and I know how it feels to be
plucked—wilting in the presence of someone who failed
to learn how to love.

Not an Ode

You give them the ~~fucking~~ handbook
and still, they can't even read.
But that's okay 'cause that just shows me
that they aren't on my feed
can't give me what I need,
and that's a shame 'cause I know me.
I'm a dying breed.
My soul, still whole, and it runs deep—

Like unexplored ocean floors.
Come and dive into my pores.
Open up these doors
and see a world, you're unawakened.
These lands are not taken,
full of color, untainted,

It's reserved for you.
Not some half-ass effort,
I don't need that noise.
I've got better things to do,
people who'll appreciate my poise.

My love, it goes unnoticed
like pennies in the street
constantly brushed under the feet
of hurried crowds—
not knowing what they're missing,
too caught up to take a bow.

You're not allowed—
into my mind without a permit.
I've been too lax letting them in,
too many, counterfeit,
such wasted time.

But all I wanted was to connect,
like a magnet or a puzzle,
a builder and architect.
Inside, I'm both,
wanting to create the perfect space
to breathe in harmony
without neglect or hidden face.

I guess it's true—
good things take time.
But I'm impatient, and you're abrasive,
it's not a match, this paradigm.

So, for this, I'm sorry.
But this one-way train is now departing.
If you find a way to pack your bags
and open up your heart
well, that's a start,
but I can't guarantee an audition for the part.

I gave you one chance,
one choice,
and one dart.

That's all I have,
just don't fall apart

Like the shadow that follows you.
And maybe I'm just hurt
'cause of the lack of follow-through.
But either way, it's true,
I need some kind of warmth
to fill these walls of mine, so blue.

Down to Ride

I might be the realist in the city,
and you might lie when people ask if you miss me.
Don't want to seem caught up in something that was,
you'd rather seem fucked up on drugs just because—
It's easier, easier than the pain,
easier than admitting you might not ever gain
what you love…
Caught up in the game, you forget to wear a glove.
Making quick love makes you feel so above
it all…

But just be careful you don't fall—
Fall behind, fall alone, fall for
someone who might never take a seat on that throne.
Fall for someone who might never give you more.
Open up the door, just to be exposed.

Armed robbery—
takes your heart from your chest, left so cold-heartedly,
and you forget just what it's like to be a part of me.
Two peas in a pod,
glued together like they were something that was
placed by God.
Oh my, but see, you're steadily losing faith,
holding on to something in your dreams, it's just a wraith.

We might've been the baddest in the city,
and you might've never had to wish

that you don't miss me.
Things change, worlds collide,
ego's shift, set aside by pride,
and sometimes, that's all it takes to decide
one was never really down for the ride.

Fatal

This man has me stressing, always has to keep me guessing
if I ever cross his mind, like he runs through mine.
The crazy thing about it all is I almost had a chance,
but I was caught up by another, sad romance.
And see, I didn't know then that he was begging for my
time.
You see, I didn't see then, it was a perfect paradigm
for everything I ever wanted.
At least, I say that now,
but the truth is that I can't even say that I know how,
or who he really is.
A fatal attraction
only led by his
mysterious way into my soul.
It's hard to let it go because I feel so consoled
by thoughts of scenarios that won't ever happen.
I'm hoping for something, without any action.
I guess I missed my shot, I guess deep inside
we didn't want to be caught—
Inside of a mess between friends and lovers.
We were secret undercovers.
Such a fatal attraction
that came to an end
before it even began.
But the look in your eyes is what got me,
that look that continues to haunt me.
I wish I could have you, it'd be such a thrill,
fatal attractions, man, do they kill.

A Seed in the Dark

Depression at its finest, but I thought I said goodbye
to the feeling deep inside of me that makes me want to
die.
But I guess it's always there, I just chose to let it go.
Somehow, I found some happiness that chose to make a
show.

Second thoughts, doubts, and questions,
but why can't you just erase
all the negative within you, and start a brand-new pace?
If I'm here and I'm willing, if I want to make it through,
why is that not enough? Why's it not enough for you?

Shit's not easy, yes I know, and baby, it may never be,
but if this is what we want, don't you dare give up on me.
'Cause I know we don't have much
but we can be all that we need,
we can be what gives the life back
to our old familiar seed.

Cloudy

Ahhh…
A breath of fresh air fills my tired lungs,
aching from the poison that is enclosed space,
close to you.
Why am I not strong enough to reject the energy you
spew?
Why do I still crave the love that to me could be so new?
Foreign, yet it's true,
I could lie down next to you,
forget just who you are
and what you come with too.
So youthful, yet so blue.
Happiness is overdue.
For you, it feels
unattainable,
forsaken.
Lost, like you.

Betrayal is a Demon

Forgiving you is easy,
it's the trust you can't regain.
The memories and the lies
weigh heavy on my brain.
You want me to forget?
How easy it must be
for you to say forget it,
scrape it all,
let's start again.
Betrayal is a demon
that laughs at me in my sleep.
I toss and turn so frequently,
but to you, it's not that deep.
"The words they all meant nothing!
I'll delete them just for you."
But the damage has been done,
and every word you spill is skewed,
the furthest from the truth.
I can't trust even a single touch
or glance that comes from you.
My word is bond.
But what the fuck is yours?
To me, it is no different
from any other whore's.

Whereunto

Maybe there's a name
for the fact that you can't blame
yourself for anything you've ever done wrong.
Maybe there's a name for the pain that doesn't leave me
while you're off and getting drunk somewhere new.
Maybe there's a name for the absence of emotion, for the
emptiness inside of your eyes.
Maybe there's a name for the reasons I can't trust you,
why the truth always tastes just like the lies.
Maybe there's a name for the way I kept on giving, even
when I felt there was nothing left to give.
And maybe there's a name for the fact that I'm still here,
even when I feel I've lost the will to live.

Drifting and pacing,
the world keeps racing,
my mind never sleeps 'cause of you.
Alone in my slumber, counting the number
of times that it takes to get through…
To you,
to you,
I'm all the way through.
I've found a way out,
Whereunto?

Begin Just to End

I love you.
Said too soon
Now we're both under the moon
Hiding faces under pillows soaked with tears.
You say that you can't eat
And I can barely feel my feet
I've been running, trembling, racing from my fears.
The end is always painful
Always dark, and dull, and mean
It's why I wish you'd never intervened.
I never wanted to begin
You always thought that we could win
But all along, I always knew we'd end up here…
Opposite ends of the sphere
Feel so far even when you're near
All it took was two years
But the damage will never be cleared.

Junior

Sometimes I feel like I'm dying,
but maybe I'm already dead.
The one I loved most is no longer,
he only exists in my head.

I'm aching in pain, it's all over,
I can't stop it now, it's too deep.
I'm spinning in circles, hungover,
can't hear me, I won't make a peep.
Silently drifting to sleep…
Eternally damned for the keep.

Hazel Eyes

I would've loved you—
with every morsel of my being,
tend to you so eagerly,
what was it you weren't seeing?
You looked for proof I had a feeling
when you should have simply asked.
We both know that people aren't the same
behind a mask.
To good at acting, I suppose,
you never knew I was imposed
by your smile and your hazel eyes,
the truth I've never yet exposed.
I guess I hid it well, tried to play it off so cool,
made you feel like we were homies
but for you, I broke all rules.
So sad, I could've loved you,
I felt you let me in,
saw the light behind your darkest walls
it all came rushing in.
But as soon as I could feel it,
I felt you pulling back.
Made me feel like it was all a dream,
just a hit-and-run attack.
I would've loved you, can't you see?
But you lost hope in all of me.
Crawled back into the comfort of your ex-girl soon to be
nothing but wasted time,
lost this pretty little dime,

now I see you drink it all away,
wash it down from 1-9.
I wish you'd let me in again,
let me love you, let this spin,
be more open with your feelings
I could always see within.

Is the love I want too deep?
Too scared to come in, dip your feet?

Sapphire Love- Split

Endless love…

My heart aches for you.

Through blood and sweat, I see no blue.

My fires rage, sapphire for you,

But yours emits a warmer hue,

A trial tried, I'm worn out too,

I longed to see the best in you.

All while my love still burns. It's true.

But my dream's my future to pursue.

Sapphire Love- Original

Endless love…

My heart aches for you.

Through blood and sweat, I see no blue.

My fires rage, sapphire for you.

But yours rests on a warmer hue.

A trial tried, I'm worn out too.

I tried to see the best in you.

But while my love is burned and true,

My dream's my future to pursue.

189

Let Go

I guess it's time for me to let go,
I never wanted to admit that I was right all along,
that I would waste a year,
be filled with slight regret, though
I could have never guessed the tides were gonna come in
that strong.

I guess it's better that we're leaving with our freedoms,
no little babies to care for,
no house to divide amongst our own.
I guess it's better that I can't say that I hate you,
'cause I was sure that'd be the end of us,
no goodbyes and no hugs.

I guess it's hard for me to let go,
I wanted nothing but forever, endless happy memories.
But such a struggle it has been from the get-go,
constantly fussing as you figure out just who you're meant
to be.

It's hard to look at you and know that you could have been
the one.
It's even harder to believe that you do love me.
But even if that's true, love can't take away the pain I feel
every time I hear your name.

This love is lost and inconsistent.
Sometimes it feels like it's in vain.

And if it feels like it's in vain, then that ain't love...

I'll keep a sweet memory,
forgive every little thing,
and even tell you I wish for you to soar.
But it's the end of you and me,
time to take off all my rings,
'cause baby, I can't fucking love you anymore.

Adaptation From a Song

I don't want to be the one you call when you're lonely, no
I want to be the one you call when you're happy

Don't want to be the one who fills your empty holes
'Cause that's not real
Not real

I'm not your savior, not your mother, not your toy
To plague with all your burdens, clean you up, and give
you joy

I will love you, but first, you need to love yourself
And that's real
Baby, so damn real

Listen here,
That's real.

Venom

Am I losing my creativity,
letting you seep into me?

The Fall

Sadly, inspiration never came,
my mind's been on a rampage trying to filter out your name.
My thoughts of you haven't been the same.
Maybe I'm just tired of feeling like this is a game.

I'm lost in you, my soul's been too attached,
bonded by the trauma, the connection is unmatched.
But here I am, looking at this latch,
ready to break the seal, open up, and light a match—

To everything inside, just burn it all away.
My heart's been reaching out for you,
you're still so far away.
I can't afford to lose another day
stuck inside a dream that was never mine to play.

I've been looking in the mirror and noticed this—
I'm not the same without you, but *without you*
is what I miss.
And even when you stretch your neck to kiss,
I can't help but feel that your actions are amiss.

I have to get away, scrape off all the glue
you've used to quickly patch between us,
trying to make us new.

There are cracks within the walls.

It's time to let go and unscrew.
Remember who I was, before I was with you.

Never Be Mine

Emptiness.
The hollowness grows deep.
Deeper than the ocean floor,
deeper than what's beneath.

Covering up emotions,
pretending they're not there.
Rejecting the sheer possibility,
you wouldn't even dare

Admit that you don't love me.
Why can't you let me go?
Stuck between revolving doors,
caught in this ebb and flow.

Is it in your nature
to hunt and prey and lie,
disguise all of the bullshit,
look me right in the eye?

Am I simply to forgive
all the "dumb" mistakes
you've made while I've been
trying, to do just what it takes

To make this love last?
Is it even real?

Or have I been a fool
that's fallen right into a trap.

Maybe love is real,
but maybe it's not this.
Maybe love is accepting
that you'll always be yours

And never be mine.

Shivers in the Night

It's so cold in here
with the absence of love.
My skin shivering, remembering the feeling of your touch.
Longingly, I reach for you in the middle of the night.
Half-asleep, I'm saying hold me,
just hoping that you might—
Love me this time,
and love me right.
That's all I ever wanted,
why's it been such a fight?
Are you scared of loving me,
scared that you just might
finally be happy
for longer than a night?

I can't fathom this—
For years on end,
you saying that you love me
but being ready to defend
yourself from every part of me
like I'm your (everlasting) enemy.
You can't get close to me
this way.

Your walls, built up so high,
you can't even recognize
you've trapped yourself where you feel most secure—
Saying that you love me

but keeping me out,
seems to me like you're still so unsure.

I wanted this to work,
wanted you to feel safe,
wanted you to let yourself go and be free.
But baby, why'd you have to hurt me?
Why'd you have to go and lie?
Ruin everything before we even got to fly.

I just hoped that you might
love me this time
and love me right.
That's all I ever wanted,
why's it been such a fight?
I think you're scared of loving me,
scared that you just might
have finally been happy,
for longer than a night.

And now we'll never know.

Reticence

Silence—
Fills the room
when there's nothing left to say.
We both know that it was never
supposed to be this way.

Home

I tried to build a home in you,
fill you with all my stuff,
I threw in all the burdens
that for me, were just too much.

I tried to set the stage,
set the future, set the pace.
I tried to build a life in you,
tried to win and beat the race.

I felt myself fall into you,
trusting maybe you'd catch on
to my idea of perfection,
us walking arm in arm.

I tried so many things with you
but again, I failed myself,
'cause while building in you
I lost the will to build myself.

I tried to build a home in you,
but that was my mistake,
'cause you're only just a man
learning how to give and take.

I'm sorry for the nails and the hammers and the bangs,
trying to build and shape you up
to an image unattained.

So retained,
I have to let it go,

pick back up the hammer
building piece by piece, but slow.

Bringing water to my garden
so it may finally grow.
Hanging art on empty walls
left neglected long ago.

Molding smiles on my face,
making sure there's room to breathe.
Realizing that
the only home I needed
was in me.

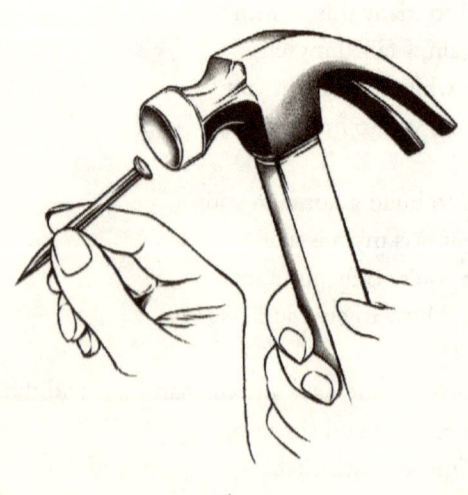

TDH

What's crazy is I would've had your babies.
I loved you so much, the truth couldn't even save me.
We would struggle, we would hustle
for the rest of our lives,
and I would barely feel love when I looked into your eyes.

No

You don't want to know…
What it is,
What I've done,
If you're still the only one…
No.

[This can't be
Don't you see
That you've been the only one for me

But you're afraid
Of the truth
You'd rather live beneath a lie

Before you can admit
That there's no fit
Between you and I
Any longer]

We must go
Before the dawn.
Before our hearts
Become confused again.

Until we fall into an endless trap…
No.
I won't let this happen one more time.

Crashed Out

I thought I knew love until I met you,
and maybe the truth is I never knew
just how far I'd take it, just how much I'd feel.
Just how everything except you felt unreal.

I gave you my life, though that didn't matter,
in the end, it's still me who's ended up shattered.
Away from my loved ones, away from the truth,
away from my beautiful, untainted youth.

I gave you my everything, wrote it in stone.
Gave you the wheel, and it cost me my bones.
Never been broken, until I met you.
Heartache was nothing, compared to this view.

Leaving you restless, while I sleep away,
mourning you under the men that I lay.
I've tried to forget, and forgive, and move on,
It's just hard to accept that our loving is gone.

I don't want to come home,
where is my home?
The place that you called ours is just catacombs,
burial grounds for the love that was sown.
Empty and soulless, my love overthrown.

Lies they still linger within all the walls,
echoing, floating, a dozen missed calls

left on my phone for when I'm not there.
You can't stand that I'm leaving,
I can no longer care.

Why should I?
When there's nothing left.
Just crimes you've committed
including the theft
of my precious heart,
woefully battered and torn straight apart.
I thought I knew love until I met you,
and maybe I convinced myself it was true—
That deep in my heart was a place just for you.
How I was mistaken, if only I knew.

Meet the Monster

I'm sorry if I've let you down,
I forgot to lock the cage.
What's inside came running out,
a monster of my pain and rage.
I swear I wasn't always like this,
never wanted to be a slave,
to emotions of my memories
I left buried in a grave.

With you, I was sweet, every time we would meet.
Now I'm wondering if all along, it was all just deceit.
I tried to let it be known,
even switched up my tone,
all in warning for the monster
that I've always known.

Your love is never something that I wanted to impede,
but love itself is always something that I've failed
to concede.

Vulnerable

I want nothing more than to be held by someone I love,
who loves me too.
But every time you touch me, it stings.
Every time I look into your eyes,
I'm reminded of a hope—
a belief that maybe
I had found someone.
Someone who could be soft enough to love me without
hurting me back, yet strong enough to withstand all my
rage, all my pain.
Maybe someone like that doesn't exist.
Maybe I should stay alone until I'm soft enough, too—
If that's even possible anymore.

Catalyst

I thought I knew what love was,
thought I practiced it at best,
thought all the love I've given
was enough to warm your chest.

But I see now that I've failed;
my love comes wrapped in poisonous spores.
Hidden beneath the surface
like sirens on a shore.

Thought I was a lover,
but I'm a catalyst at best,
forcing a reaction,
painful to digest.

Everyone I've tried to love
ends up tattered
and obsessed.
I guess it isn't love I give,
I guess I'm just a mess.

Spoiled Mess

Sometimes I wonder if I'm spoiled,
the way I handle your love.
Greeting soft kisses with blades,
but expecting your touch to always be soft,
demanding that it never fades—
Even when I hurt you.

How is it that I grew up starved of love?
And now, somehow, I'm spoiled.
Drinking and drinking, I'll drown in your love,
and still say that it's not enough.

What is it about you I can't seem to grasp?
What is it that just doesn't sit—
right on my conscience?
Deep inside me,
it's never been quite the right fit.

Our bodies are tangled,
our words become mush,
I'm spinning right out of my head.
I said I was ready, but maybe I wasn't.
I should've just left you on read.

Out of my head, out of my head,
you only belonged in my bed.
I fear I've betrayed you,
fear I've misled,

all the words that I've spoken are dead.

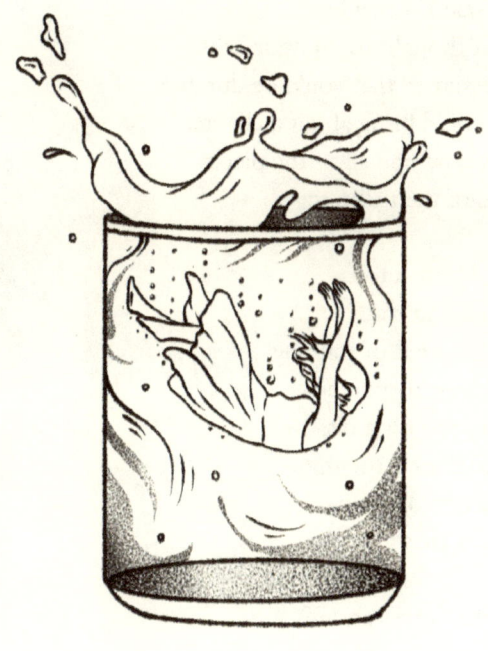

Fixer-Uppers

Yet again, my feelings have somewhere gone.
But I can't say I'm surprised.
As much as it ails me,
this is a familiar song.
Forever longing to be captured,
in just the right light,
I've never had someone who could hold me
without me taking flight—

Again, into the air,
which thickens as I fly.
I always said I'd be a bird;
you never thought to question why.
Always assumed that you'd be different,
that you could bring about a change,
and somehow find all of the pieces
of my heart, then rearrange.

In truth, I hoped too
that it could be you.
'Cause I get tired of running,
always with someone new.
It's always fun for a bit,
until I see right through
every last one of them.
Oh, what a view!

Is that what love's about?

Constantly being disappointed?
Or is it the act of accepting
Every. Single. Flaw?
'Cause if it's either, I'll be truthful—
I'm better off alone.
This world has enough flaws,
and I can be bad all on my own.

Or very good; both are true.
I'm a happy person, too.
Until a man comes knocking on my door,
ruining my view.

They never quite offer me
what I need yet beg to stay.
Instead of letting me enjoy
and build my life, they come to play.

Bringing all their baggage
and their worries and their shame.
Hoping I can fix them,
patch them up and make them sane.

I'm tired of all these fixer-uppers coming to my door,
asking me for love when they can't even learn to pour—
straight into me, they just spill and make a mess,
then blame me for the trouble—
their failed attempt at success
in winning me over and gaining a wife.
All I did was take them in after they begged...
It's not alright.

213

I'm tired of having my precious peace disturbed.
If there's nothing you can offer me without making me feel free,
then your best bet is to reconsider trying to love me.

A Duel in Duality

Sometimes I wonder why life is cruel,
Why it feels like I'm battling an endless duel

Between myself and the self that I am,
Hoping whoever wins isn't a sham.

I'm getting older, and it's hard to admit
I'm scared of aging, just a little bit.

Too much love to be alone, too much freedom to commit,
Am I really just a hypocrite?

I said I loved you, and it warmed your heart,
But you didn't know it was the hardest part

To say the words I knew I couldn't hold,
Laid a card out on the table, just to fold.

I wish I knew why life was cruel,
Wish I had the proper fuel

To nourish my discouraged soul,
Give me strength until I feel whole.

You're just the kind I'd always hoped to find,
Sweet and thoughtful, well designed.

Who would've thought you'd be placed in my view,
Ready and willing to start anew.

I always knew that life was cruel,
Never thought I'd end up the fool.

Poured all my love into a black hole
Lost in time, now I've lost control.

If only sooner, you and I had met,
When I was willing to take the bet

That love existed and could weather all storms,
Push against evil, denude all forms.

Now I question my take on love,
Question whether it's fake that love,

Question whether I have it in my heart
Left to give, when I'm torn apart.

I tell you sweetly that life is cruel,
'Cause if it wasn't, I'd end this duel,

Put down my sword and run to you,
Forever saying I love you.

Withered

Winter came and buried the flowers we worked so hard to grow.
And when spring came, not a budding bloom survived the vicious snow.

Empty

How does it feel so empty
To lie here next to you?
When all I want to do is love
The vessel that is you.

The Ages

Why have I been running for so long?
What from, where to, how long?

I feel the bricks on my back and the splinters in my toes...
but I don't know where to go.

11 years old
I thought maybe I loved you.
In fact, I almost knew I did.
But in truth, I never even knew you.
Just something I made up in my head.
Too scared to say I'd be yours. Afraid I'd mess it up.
Like fear of being abandoned.
But who abandoned me before?

14 years old
I found someone to love.
New for me to be so close to someone.
To wake up every day and see you there, close my eyes,
and see you there again.
I wore that ring you gave me on my finger.
Holding on to this thought of forever.
Three years I gave to you so blindly.
How I wish I knew.

17 years old
The cycle starts again.
This time, I'm more experienced,

less inclined to fall in love.
I say no the first time you ask.
I needed more time, but slowly, you melted into me.
Seeped and deepened, I experienced something different.
Exciting for me, new for you.
I playfully gave you my love, but your trust wasn't given,
so insecure, you wanted something more.

24 years old
New city, new me.
You plunged headfirst, no breaks.
Still haunted by my past, not looking for love.
You tickled me into submission.
To say yes, you pulled my strings.
Tugged on my heart, it beats.
There's life inside of me.
So high you got off me.
So much in such little time.
But I never felt it was real.
Felt I gave too much.
So, I ran and ran and ran.
Running and running some more.
Running and running and running.
But what from and what to?

What led me to you?
Is love even true?

Rattle Me

Have I always been afraid of love,
as badly as I've craved it?
Who knew a heart so big
could be diluted under fear.

What's more, I've been numbed,
with poisoned lies from your tongue,
that made it hard to recognize my own volition.

Months without you near,
can't say I've missed you in my ear.
In fact, I'm glad I finally found my way to something more
sincere.

Thank you for the years
I will never get back.
You rattled me right where I needed to be.

On the Corner of Burbank and Tyrone

So quickly things change,
like winter to summer overnight.
You'd think there'd be a warning light,
and maybe there was.

It's like you're crashing into me
and I feel it happening
but I can't say stop
and mean it.

You feel like a magnet
pulling me in.
I've never felt that way before.
And I can't say I have feelings, yet
but I know that I want more,
and you don't want me to walk out that door.

One taste, and you didn't want me to leave.
To tell you the truth, that might scare me.
Just don't move too fast.

Gentle kisses all over,
me asleep in your bed
with just two nights of spending time with you.
That never happens.

I'm reserved when it comes to love,
open when it comes to sex,

and somehow, you skipped right over sex,
right over my walls.

I was nervous,
but seeing you made me calm,
or maybe I'm just a great actress.

Just don't move too fast
or you'll scare me away,
I know this all too well.

Intuition

You trace your fingers down my spine,
admiring my design,
hoping that with time
you'll soon enough be mine.

Leave me messages each day,
"Goodnight," "Good morning," "How's your day?"
And always miss me when I'm somewhere far away.

You love to please me every chance you get,
appease me when I start to fret,
and gift me with the smallest acts of care.

You always listen till I fall asleep
and hold me when I feel weak,
and treat me in a way that's kind and fair.

I sometimes wonder who you *really* are,
question if you're really true,
and ask myself just how it is that I've found you.

I guess there's nothing I can do
except accept that this is you,
and hope that everything you've given me is true.

Subscribe

By August I knew that I loved you,
this much I know is true.
Despite all the denial
I'm at peace when I'm with you.

What started as a magnet
dipped in curiosity,
shifted to a darted vision,
a future both of us could see.

I know that I'm not ready,
but I truly want to be,
so that I may give you all this love
harbored inside of me.

You give me a new feeling,
one I'm struggling to describe.
All I know is that I like it,
count me in, I have subscribed.

Inspiration

Just when I've lost inspiration,
here comes you.
Like new colors on a sunrise,
golden hue.

Except I'm looking through a window,
can't feel the crisp air,
can't see you in your glory,
can't feel you bare.

She's stuck on you,
what can we do?
It's wrong for me to think of you,
but here I am—
An endless night
thinking only of you
and wishing I could feel you.

This is Ecstasy

Wet

My stomach ripples and waves
in rage and hollowness.
I am hungry.
But not just for a bite to eat.
I am hungry,
for affection and love.
Not just any love,
romantic love is what I crave,
to keep my raging soul at bay,
to be kissed and touched, tenderly
and sleep inside your arms.
The heat of your skin
surrounding me,
My love.

To hear a whisper
in the middle of the night
tickling in my ear,
telling me I'm loved and wanted
as the moon peeks through the window
to watch us play.

Yes, what a dream
so many men
have tried to create.
But there is only
One—
in which I crave.

So sad,
for we've not met.
A glimpse inside a fantasy
I've played to make me
wet.

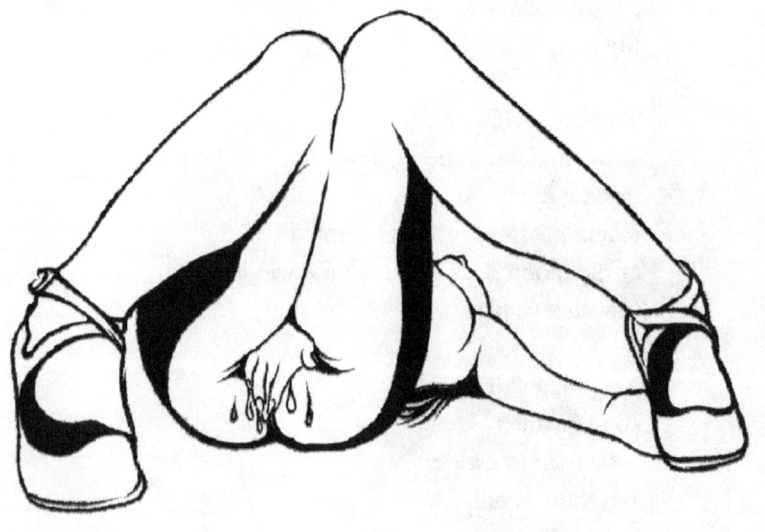

Lust

It's times like these I find myself eager for your skin.
'Cause no one touches quite like you,
pleasing me with sin.
I know that all it'd take for you to show up at my door,
is just a simple word from me, saying I need more

Memories of ecstasy,
bodies intertwined,
biting, kissing, scratching,
hair pulling from behind.

But sadly, it was all a dream,
A transient former life.
One that I cannot relive,
fate sealed in a knife.

But how I wish to find another,
teach them what you knew
about just how to please my flesh
and make me feel new.
And how I know that no one ever
could do what you do,
'cause you were much too ardent,
but the love you had was blue.

Blue, so blue, hotter than any red.
The passion in your soul would flood in me,
I'd soak the bed.

Legs shaking, pulse fleeting,
again, again, again.
Again, is all I'd want from you
again, again, again.

We'd be caught up for hours,
you'd love the way I'd moan.
I'd love the way you'd look at me,
just after you'd been blown.

Again, again, again
Wait. Stop. No. Please.
The words slip out my mouth,
my eyes still fixed on yours,
your face headed down south,
avoiding all detours.

My teeth pressed on my lips,
my head, falling backwards,
your hands gripped on my hips,
awaiting the rewards.

The memories, these images,
they're lodged inside my mind.
An echo in my brain,
constantly playing on rewind.

It's times like these I need
just a simple helping hand.
One who will agree
to follow my command.

Tantalize

They call me tantalizing,
hypnotizing,
but I really don't know why
when it's just them fantasizing
about what they think I am,
maybe how they think I feel.
It was never in my plan
to become something so real
in your imagination—

Baby, take a seat,
you've been working all day,
let me get you off your feet.
Lay you down on the bed,
give you something to eat—
Yes, I'm talking 'bout the head,
'cause I know you like it sweet.

Mmmm, let's take turns,
let me give you a nice treat,
have you feeling so relaxed,
I won't stop till you release—
but oh, snap back,
I'm not even in your sheets.
I've been playing in your mind,
you haven't even had a piece.

He says I'm tantalizing,
hypnotizing,
but I really don't know why—

Would You Let Me?

If I gave you no choice,
if I had you alone, if you just heard my voice

Would you let me?
If I just kissed your lips,
if I had you alone, if you just felt my hips

Would you let me?
If I just pushed you down,
if I had you alone, if I lifted my gown

Would you let me?
If I pulled off your clothes,
if I had you alone, if the tension arose

Would you let me? If I just climbed on top,
if I had you alone, if I just wouldn't stop

Would you let me? If you felt it inside,
if I had you alone, if I started to ride

Would you let me? If I shouted your name,
if I had you alone, if I suddenly came

Would you let me? If I just made you cum,
if I had you alone, if your body felt numb

Would you let me?

Or is there no need to ask,
'cause I have you alone,
but I'm dying to ask...

Will you let me?

In Bloom

You were too afraid to take me,
I'd be patient, baby.
You just looked at me like you had never seen
A woman
In bloom—
A woman,
Naked in your room.
Yes, a woman, mmmm
Flesh kissed by the moon.

Let me be your escape.
Drown inside me, leave your sorrows—
Deep inside my ocean walls
There exists no tomorrows.

So blue,
Your sorrows,
Betrayed by you so soon.
Tangled up, enraptured, by this web of pure desire.
Tickled hairs and no despairs,
Just fumes of ardor burning,
Your stomach slowly churning
From this woman,
In bloom—
Waiting still for you.

Don't pretend to look the other way,
I know you'll take me soon.

The longer that you wait,
The sweeter the fruit will taste,
Ripened in your face—
This woman
In bloom—
Take me
To the moon, the moon, the moon.

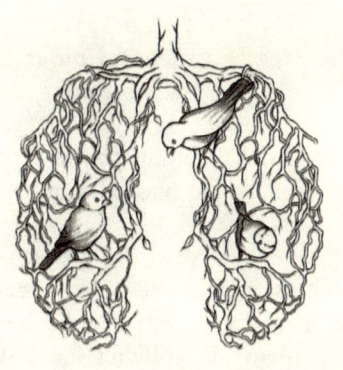

Acknowledgments

To my parents, who gave me life and continue to love me every day, I will always be grateful for your sacrifices.

To my sister, who's inspired so much in me, and who I hope to always be a safe space for, you'll always have a friend in me.

To my grandparents, who've shaped me in more ways than they know, I hold every memory dearly.

To my friends who feel like family, you've kept me going through the years, and I'm so blessed to have found you in this lifetime.

To everyone who's loved me—every partner and relationship I've had—thank you for the love and the lessons. Without them, I wouldn't have found the inspiration to write.

And to those of you who support me and have been with me on my journey as I navigate life, thank you. It never goes unnoticed.

I love you all.

About the Author

Alexandria has lived a dynamic and multifaceted life, weaving her experiences into an ever-evolving artistic journey. While her career has taken her through many roles, art has always been her constant—a vital thread that connects her to the human experience. Over the years, she has explored countless creative mediums, including music, dance, photography, modeling, acting, singing, painting, and writing.

Her love for storytelling began in childhood, when she wrote short stories that earned recognition and encouragement from her teachers. By the age of 11, she discovered poetry as her most natural form of expression—a way to process her experiences and give voice to her thoughts and emotions. Since then, she has been writing consistently, making it a personal goal to create at least one piece each month.

With a background in psychology and graphic design, Alexandria's curiosity is as boundless as her creativity. She is deeply inspired by philosophical questions and the intricacies of the human condition, which often shape her poetry. Her adventurous spirit keeps her exploring new experiences, many of which find their way into her writing.

Alexandria pours vulnerability onto the page, writing with unrestrained honesty and introspection. Her poetry delves into the complexity of human emotions, exploring themes of sorrow, longing, fragility, and connection
while confronting the weight of depression and the harsh realities of an imperfect world. Balancing dreamlike abstraction with raw intensity, her words evoke a visceral response, capturing the essence of human existence.

Outside of writing, Alexandria can be found planning her next adventure, dancing freely in her room, or spending quality time with the people she loves. She dreams of one day working as a creative director, furthering her education, and establishing her own psychological practice—all while continuing to explore the limitless possibilities of art and creativity.

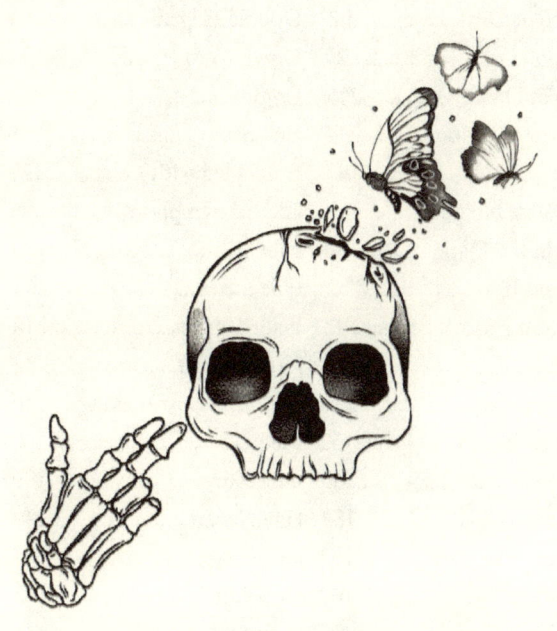

Index

www.ingramcontent.com/pod-product-compliance
Lightning Source LLC
Chambersburg PA
CBHW021716120626
46545CB00004B/1586